# DESTROYERMAN

# DESTROYERMAN

Kenny Sams

gatekeeper press™

Tampa, Florida

Published by Gatekeeper Press
7853 Gunn Hwy., Suite 209
Tampa, FL 33626
www.GatekeeperPress.com



Library of Congress Control Number:

ISBN (hardcover): 9781662954870
ISBN (paperback): 9781662954887
eISBN: 9781662954894

# Dedication

This book is dedicated to all the destroyermen who served before me and set the standard to *be* a destroyerman. I thank you for the legacy you left me. Also, to the destroyermen who followed after me. I hope I left the same standard for you to follow. This book is also dedicated to all the destroyermen who never returned home. You paid the ultimate price, my brothers, and I personally am damn proud of you for your sacrifice. Thank you from the bottom of my heart.

# Contents

# Foreword

Every veteran has "stories." Some veterans share them, some don't. Some share "some" of them while keeping the bad ones to themselves. I've always shared some of my stories with my daughters (five of them), but there are some they'll never hear.

One day I was sharing one of my stories with one of my daughters, and she asked me why I didn't write them down.

My answer to her was, "Nobody would want to hear them."

She said, "I do, and so does your grandson."

I thought about this and realized that I wished my grandpa and dad had written down "their" stories.

My grandpa was born in 1881, and my dad was born in 1918, and they both had fascinating stories that I loved listening to. My grandpa traveled out west in a covered wagon when he was a young boy, and my dad traveled with a carnival during the thirties and forties. They were both "full" of stories.

Everyone says, "Someday I'm going to write a book." Very few actually do. I'm pushing seventy now, and my memories are starting to fade. I'm writing them down now, before they disappear. My children and grandchildren will be left with at least "some" documentation of my life.

There's an old joke in the navy that goes like, "Do you know the difference between a sea story and a fairy tale?" A fairy tale starts with, "Once upon a time," and a sea story starts with, "This is no shit."

My stories are as truthful as I can remember them. I will not use last names, except in very positive instances. I don't want to offend anyone. I just want to tell the story.

What is a destroyer? Destroyers—also affectionately known as "tin cans," "greyhounds," and "frigates"—are small ships that were developed to screen larger ships with less maneuverability, such as battleships and aircraft carriers. They're highly maneuverable and fast. They're well armed and extremely versatile. Being a smaller ship, they're capable of operating in water that would be too shallow for the larger heavier ships. The downside to this is that they're some of the "roughest riding" of the navy ships; the only ships rougher would be minesweepers, tugs, or gunboats.

What is a "destroyerman?" He is the sailor that mans these little ships. He's the bluejacket that can fall asleep anyplace, anytime, instantly, but will be awake and alert within seconds. He's the sailor who can walk down a passageway with his feet on the deck one second, and on the bulkhead the next when the ship takes a roll. He's the sailor who's as much at home handling lines as he is fighting fires. He's the sailor leaving the messdecks with a banana in one pocket and an apple in the other "for later." He's the guy who can go days without sleep and still be alert. He's the one who can endure months at sea and is a master at passing time. He's the sailor I want watching my back.

My time in the United States Navy was the greatest time of my life. It was an adventure that spanned two decades. I was able to see and experience things the average person can only dream about. It was also a learning experience. I learned humility, honor, pride, friendship, and brotherhood. It made me the man I am today. I also learned that the world isn't always a nice place. There's a lot of "bad" out there, and our lives here in the States are pretty good, despite what some would say. Believe me, we've got it good.

I'm not sure how many countries I visited on my deployments. Every time I try to count them, I come up with different numbers—I always seem to forget some. But suffice it to say that I traveled all over the Pacific Ocean, the Indian Ocean, and the Middle East. All along Africa, Indonesia, Australia, and as far north as the Aleutian Islands, even close to the coastline of Russia. I got to travel all over the United States and even down to Mexico. It's a big world out there, and there's a *lot* of *ocean*. I not only logged thousands upon thousands of miles aboard ship, but also by air. I had the *pleasure* of crossing the Pacific several times on military cargo planes, usually in pursuit of one of my ships, or trying to get home on emergency leave for one tragedy or another.

Why do men go to sea? They have for thousands of years. Is it the pursuit of adventure? Is it out of curiosity? Is it to seek solitude? There are many, many reasons, but I feel it's mainly just a love of the sea. It's a beautiful, peaceful place, most of the time. But when it's not, it can be overwhelming and terrifying. Ask any mariner who's been through a hurricane or typhoon. With today's modern ships, the risks are fewer than, say, two hundred years ago, but they're still there to some extent.

To whoever reads these stories, I hope you enjoy them. If you're an old "destroyerman" like me, I hope you can relate, and if I get something wrong, please forgive me. I'm trying to remember as best I can. If you're a civilian with no knowledge of the navy, I hope you find the stories enlightening and entertaining. If you're an old shipmate of mine, I hope they jog your memory and help you remember "way back when."

*Anchors aweigh, shipmates!*

# Prologue

As I said before, my time in the navy was the greatest time of my life. I'm a lot older now, and a lot of life has gone by. My children are all grown and have kids of their own. I'm even a great-grandfather now. I have much more life behind me than I do ahead of me, and I thank God for the life I've had.

After being discharged from the navy, I pursued a civilian career in industrial maintenance. My navy training and experience gave me the skills, electrically and mechanically, to repair and maintain industrial machinery. Let's face it—there are no gun mounts or weapons systems in the civilian world. I became a millwright. I continued to learn more skills, such as welding and metal fabrication, and did pretty well.

Early on in my civilian career, my supervisory skills were recognized by my employers, skills that I learned in my naval career, and I moved up quickly in my career field. My last position before I retired was as plant engineer for a food processing company. All my skills, I can honestly say, were attributed to my naval service. As a civilian millwright, I worked for an aluminum mill, a steel mill, a plastic recycling company, a Popsicle plant, a machinery manufacturing company, and a food processing plant. I learned something from all of them, but none of it came even close to the navy.

There *is* one thing that stands out to me about civilian jobs. Everywhere I worked, it was "dog-eat-dog." I don't remember there being any rivalry or petty jealousies in the navy. Everyone worked together as a team and got along. In the civilian world, it seemed that I always had to watch my back. It's a pity. There was always someone who would try to undermine someone else to gain "points." What a way to get ahead in a job.

When I joined the navy, my brother-in-law, who'd served in the army and Vietnam during Tet, gave me some advice.

He said, "Before you leave home, take a serious look around, and plant it in your memory."

"Why?" I asked.

"Because you'll never be able to come back to it as you left it," he said.

He was absolutely right. After I left, then went back home on leave, everything had changed; even my high school friends seemed different. I'm not sure what changed, whether it was home or me. I'm pretty sure it was the latter. I think I had somehow grown inside. I passed this same advice on to my youngest daughter, who decided to join the navy after high school. She's still in the navy and is now a senior chief petty officer. I'm damn proud of her.

Many, many years have passed since I first set foot on board a ship and walked a rolling, pitching deck or watched porpoises playing in the ship's wake, but those days have stayed with me throughout my life, and I visit them on a daily basis.

I don't think there's a sailor alive who doesn't do the same thing. I have a shirt that one of my daughters gave me that pretty much sums it up. It says: "Vietnam, I was there. Sometimes I still am." It's my favorite shirt.

I want to thank you, dear reader, for listening to my stories. I hope you enjoy them as much as I've enjoyed writing them.

# CHAPTER ONE

# The Beginning

In 1968, I joined the US Naval Sea Cadets at the age of fourteen. Little did I know how much it would change my life.

As a sea cadet, I was able to experience many things that were not available to me as a "civilian." I was allowed access to military bases, military training, and in particular, navy ships.

We were issued regular navy uniforms—just like the "real" sailors—only our insignia was different. Plus, we wore shoulder patches that said, "US Naval Sea Cadets." I'm sure the real sailors thought we were "wannabes," which we were. Some probably thought we were "cute."

The unit I was attached to met every two weeks at the Naval Reserve Center in Stockton, California. We met for about three hours on a weeknight—don't remember which one—but during these meetings, we received naval training from navy volunteers that were stationed at the reserve center.

The training covered just about everything that a regular sailor is trained in. From military ceremonies and protocol, basic seamanship, shipboard firefighting, basic gunnery, signaling, the code of conduct, you name it—if it was navy, we were taught it.

As I said, we were taught by regular navy sailors. One instructor I remember in particular was Gunner's Mate First Class Evans. He was my favorite. It's funny. I was to run into him many years later when I was a chief petty officer and he was a master chief petty officer.

I went to the Mobile Technical Unit in Pearl Harbor, Hawaii, to get help with a technical problem we were having with our gun system, and whom did I need to talk to . . . Master Chief Evans! The navy is actually a pretty small community, and I've had many instances of running into ex-shipmates over the years, even as a civilian.

One of the perks of being a sea cadet was that we got to go on navy vessels. We were bussed to Alameda Naval Air Station to attend two weeks of aircraft familiarization, which was fun, but we also got to go aboard and tour the USS *Oriskany*, a navy aircraft carrier. *Impressive* is too weak of a word for it.

One time we got to spend about five days on board the USS *San Joaquin County*, an old LST (landing ship, tank), as it cruised up the Sacramento River from San Francisco to Stockton. That was quite an experience for a teenage boy. It was my first time being on a ship that was actually "underway," even though it wasn't at sea. The crew treated us like we were part of them, and it helped cement my desire to be a sailor.

After my sophomore year in high school, in the summertime, we had the opportunity to go to navy "boot camp." It was a two-week trip, and the navy flew us down to San Diego on a navy P-3. It was my first time flying, and what an experience.

When we landed in San Diego, they loaded us onto a navy bus and took us to the Recruit Training Center. There were about eight of us from the Stockton unit, and we were combined with other sea cadets from other units in the Bay Area. Altogether, there were about thirty of us to form a "company."

It was a wonderful experience for me. We spent a lot of time in classes, learning everything that the regular sailors were taught. We were taught NBC warfare (nuclear, biological, and chemical); they even had us go through the "gas chamber." The gas chamber was a building where you were taught how to use a gas mask. They taught us how to don them. Then we had to put them on, enter the gas chamber, stand in ranks inside, and they would fill the chamber with tear gas. We stood there for a few minutes, and then they had us remove our gas masks. Wow, I don't ever want to experience that again. It took hours for my eyes to stop burning, but it did teach me the importance of gas masks.

They also taught us basic firefighting skills. After the classroom lessons, they took us to the firefighting "mockup," assigned us to "hose teams," had us don OBAs (oxygen-breathing apparatus), and had us put out a fire, which was in a huge tank and consisted of burning JP-5 fuel. *Hot* is the only way I can describe it.

We were also taught "survival at sea." I really enjoyed it because it was hot in San Diego, and survival was taught in a swimming pool. The whole idea behind it was how to stay afloat if you're "lost at sea." They taught us how to use our clothing as floatation devices, including our "white hats." The technique was to trap air in our clothes and use it to keep ourselves buoyant. Besides that, the cool water was so refreshing. We had to jump into a swimming pool fully clothed in our dungarees and stay afloat for, I believe, an hour (it might have been more). This was a very long time ago, and my memory isn't what it used to be.

First aid was also on the agenda. Not just simple first aid but combat first aid. Abdominal wounds, chest wounds, arterial bleeding, broken bones, CPR—just about everything a sailor could need.

One of the most memorable things they taught us was "laundry." We had to wash our clothes in buckets of cold water. They had these huge concrete tables out behind the barracks that we washed our clothes on, then we would hang them on the clothesline with "clothes stops" (these were pieces of small cotton line about eight inches long). We had to tie our clothes to the clothesline, then post a watch—"clothesline watch." I thought it was ridiculous to have to stand watch on laundry, but as I was to learn, the navy has a reason for everything.

Everywhere we went, we marched in formation. Whether it was to another training exercise or to chow. March, march, march. If there were only two or three of us, we still had to march in formation. We weren't allowed to go anywhere alone unless we had a "walking chit" (a slip of paper with signed permission, much like a hall pass in school) signed by our company commander. Our company commander was pretty cool. I remember he was a chief signalman, and we were his last company; he was retiring as soon as we were done.

We were taught how to handle mooring lines on board the USS *Neversail*. It was a mock-up of a small ship. We were taught how to use heaving lines, the proper way to secure the mooring lines to the bits, and how to frap lines.

My favorite was the rifle and pistol range. The largest gun I had ever shot was a .22 caliber. At the range, we were taught how to handle and fire an M1 rifle (.30 caliber) and a 1911-A1 .45 caliber pistol. I fell in love with it.

I don't know of anyone during my career who ever said they enjoyed boot camp, but I did. When school started again that fall, and my high school buddies asked what I did over the summer, I just said, "Oh, not much. I flew down to San Diego and went to navy boot camp."

The third time I got to go aboard ship was a two-week trip on the coast guard cutter *Taney*. She was homeported out of Alameda, California.

We went aboard and got underway for Astoria, Oregon. I believe we were underway for about five days before we pulled into Astoria. It was a fantastic new world for me. It was my first time out on the ocean, and I fell in love with it. I decided then that this was what I wanted to do with my life.

I spent the bulk of my time up on the signal bridge because I wanted to become a signalman when I joined the navy in the future. The signalmen were really cool and wonderful mentors, and they taught me as much as they could in such a short period of time. They taught me semaphore, flag hoist, and as much Morse code as I could remember.

Life aboard ship is pretty much the same, whether it's a coast guard ship or a navy ship. The routine is the same: wake up at reveille, eat breakfast, assemble for quarters in the morning, turn to for ships work, lunch, turn to again until knock-off (quitting time of ship's work) in the afternoon, about an hour of free time, then supper, another hour or so of free time, watch the movie on the messdecks, then turn in at "taps." It doesn't vary much from that, unless they have drills during the day, which is just about every day (man-overboard drills, general quarters drills, loss of steering drills, fire drills, etc.).

They even had us standing watches: bridge watches, lookout watches, and engineering watches. In fact, the *Taney* was the first ship where I learned how to be a helmsman. I was also taught lee helmsman, messenger of the watch, and lookout.

The one thing that impressed me the most was the sea. It was so vast, beautiful, and so powerful. The sunrises and sunsets were breathtaking. It really made a person feel small. Also, there was the smell of the ocean and the movement of the ship under your feet, a slow roll and pitch. The horizon was unbroken, a flat line in every direction.

Again, I knew then that I wanted to spend my life as a sailor.

We pulled into Astoria, moored to a pier downtown, and were allowed to go ashore on liberty. I remember setting foot on shore and having a little difficulty walking straight. I had my first set of "sea legs." (It wears off after a day or so. That's why sailors have a certain swagger when they walk after being at sea for a period of time. Compensating for the roll and pitch of the ship, when that roll and pitch isn't there anymore, the brain still tries to compensate.)

Liberty in Astoria wasn't much fun, not much for a teenage boy to do. All the sailors from the ship went to the bars, but we were too young, so we mostly hung out on the ship.

After a couple of days, the ship got underway again to head back to Alameda. The return trip was pretty much the same as the trip up. More training and more watches. I had the time of my life.

I stayed in the sea cadets until I turned seventeen in 1971. When I did, I made a decision that I wanted to drop out of school to join the navy. Boy, that didn't go over very well with my mom. She hit the ceiling.

High school was a mess. I was in my junior year, we were having race riots at school, I wasn't learning anything, and everyone was afraid all the time. I was just fed up with it. I wanted to get out of there. I even started cutting school so I wouldn't have to deal with it. I was never prejudiced, but apparently, a lot of my classmates were.

My dad was an awesome man. I had a long talk with him one evening about how I was feeling and what I wanted to do with my life. He listened and actually heard what I was saying. A couple days later, he pulled me aside and asked me if I was *absolutely* sure of what I wanted to do.

"Yes, Dad, I am," was my reply.

He said, "I talked to your mom, and we're willing to let you go."

I can't express how that made me feel. I was going into the navy!

This was in October of 1971. I had no idea how complicated it was to join the navy at seventeen.

First, I had to get a GED, since I hadn't graduated from high school. That was a lengthy process. It took me a few weeks, but I finally finished it. Then I had to take some aptitude tests for the navy, to see what job skills I had and what rating I was qualified for. When the scores came back, my recruiter told me that I was qualified for any rating I wanted. I told him I wanted to be a gunner's mate, just like Petty Officer Evans at the Reserve Center.

He looked at me with an expression of surprise and told me, "Do you have any idea what gunner's mates do?"

I told him, "Of course I do."

He said with a sigh, "Well, if you're sure."

So that sealed it—I was going to be a gunner's mate.

Then my dad had to sign for me. I don't remember my recruiter's name. All I remember is that he was an electrician's mate first class. He was a very honest man and did everything he could to help me get what I wanted. Since I had been in the sea cadets, he recruited me as an E-3 (or "seaman"), and since I had attended two weeks of boot camp while in the sea cadets, I wasn't required to go through that in the navy. I already knew everything they would teach me, which I thought was pretty awesome.

So the deal was sealed. I was finished with the recruiting phase and ready to "ship out." I was given a bus ticket and was to report to the induction center in Oakland, California, on January 31, 1972. I arrived at the induction center with ten dollars in my pocket and the clothes on my back.

Anyone who has ever been in the military can tell you what an induction center is like. It's an all-day process, and you're in your underwear most of the time. You stand in line for everything. It's a mass physical exam. The only break we got was at lunchtime. We were all given meal vouchers and sent down the street to an automated cafeteria that had crappy food. The best depiction of an induction center I've ever seen is in the movie *Alice's Restaurant*.

After I was finished, we were herded into a room, stood in ranks, and were sworn in. I had finally become a real sailor.

The next step was more waiting while they created my service record and wrote up my orders. When they *finally* called my name, I was handed my service record, my orders, a bus token, and a piece of paper with directions to Treasure Island Naval Station, where I was to complete my processing.

I checked in to the admin building, gave them my orders, and was given a "check-in sheet." The first thing on the "check-in sheet" was the transient barracks. I found it and "checked in."

I was given a wool blanket, pillow, pillowcase, and a couple of sheets and was assigned a bunk.

The barracks were huge. I found my assigned bunk—a "bottom" bunk, which was good—made my bed, and was all set. Then I went back down to the office to get directions to the mess hall, got some pretty good supper, then headed back to the barracks and went to bed. I was there! I was so excited that night I hardly slept at all. *I was in the navy.*

The next morning, I woke up at about 0830, went down to the barracks office to find out what I was supposed to do and where I was supposed to go, and was told, "You're on report!"

I was flabbergasted. "What am I on report for?" I asked.

"You're on report for being UA," I was told.

"What do you mean 'UA'?" I replied.

"You were supposed to muster at 0800."

Nobody told me this when I checked in the day before. He handed me a sheet of paper that had the rules of the barracks on it, and sure enough, there it was, "Muster: 0800." I was devastated. My first day in the navy and I was already in trouble.

My next place to check in was administration. I had to fill out so many forms. They took my picture, issued me an ID card, and sent me on my way.

Then the next stop was "uniform issue." When I got there, they gave me another form to fill out that asked for my clothing sizes. I filled it out, gave it back to them, then waited about an hour. They finally called me up to the window and handed me a *ton* of uniforms and a seabag. It probably took me close to an hour to get all the uniforms in the seabag. Then I had to carry them across the base to the barracks. Finally, when I got there, I stashed my uniforms in my locker, changed into my uniform, and then went on to my next "check-in." At this point I finally felt like a *sailor*.

My next check-in was at the dispensary. They did a more thorough physical, then gave me a bunch of shots. Then it was on to the barbershop for a "military" haircut. The rest of the check-in process was pretty much the same. They assigned me to a duty section, so every fourth day, I had to stand duty, which mostly consisted of standing watch in one of the administration or command buildings. If it wasn't my duty day, I was allowed to leave the base at 1530. I got to see a lot of San Francisco. For some reason, my favorite was Chinatown.

On the third day, I went down to the barracks office to muster. During roll call, when he called my name and I answered, the petty officer in charge told me I had to change into my dress uniform and report to the command building for "captain's mast" at 1000.

"Why do I have to go to captain's mast?" I asked.

"Because you missed muster the other day," was the answer.

I was terrified. Not three days in the navy and I was already in trouble.

I went back to my locker, changed into my dress uniform, and just sat there for the longest time, trying to think of what I was going to say to the captain.

At 1000 I was at the command building. I was directed to take a seat in a hallway with about six other sailors. Finally, a master-at-arms came out and gave us directions for when we were in front of the captain. Then, wouldn't you know it, I was the first one to be called in.

I stood at attention in front of the captain as he read the charge against me. Then he paused for a long time while he was looking at my service record.

Finally, he asked me, "Seaman Sams, how long have you been in the navy?"

"Three days, sir," was my reply.

Then he asked me if I had an explanation.

"Nobody told me I had to muster, sir," was my answer.

I could tell it was all he could do to keep from laughing. Instead, he told me to use this as a lesson about being where you're supposed to be when you're supposed to be there. Then he wished me luck in my navy career and dismissed the charges. What a relief. I never missed another muster during my entire naval career.

One of the things I noticed was that they had beer machines in the barracks. For fifty cents, you could have a cold beer whenever you wanted it. I was only seventeen, but that didn't stop me from putting my fifty cents into that machine that evening, just to celebrate that the charges were dropped against me. Then I put another fifty cents in, then another, and then another. The next morning, I woke up with the worst headache I'd ever had.

During my stay there, I had to make one more trip to the dispensary for even more shots. The navy sure likes to give a lot of shots. You get used to it. This time all was well. I went to supper, watched some TV in the barracks lounge, then started feeling really tired, so I went to bed. I'm not sure what time it was, but in the middle of the night, I woke up with a fever, was sweating, and started vomiting. I couldn't even get out of bed. I was pretty out of it.

One of the other guys went down and got the duty petty officer, who called the base ambulance. They showed up, put me on a stretcher, and hauled me to the dispensary. Once there, they gave me another shot of something, and in a little while, I started feeling better.

As it turned out, one of the shots they had given me the day before was a typhoid shot. I was allergic to it. After a couple of hours, I was feeling good enough to go back to the barracks and get some sleep. I also had a "no-duty chit" and a "rack pass," which allowed me to stay in bed the next morning. By the end of the next day, I was pretty much back to normal.

Finally, the day came when I went down to morning muster. The leading petty officer told me that I was to report to the admin building immediately after muster. I hurried over there and reported in, and they told me that my orders were in. They were just finishing them up, and I was free to depart as soon as I had them in my hand. I had been at Treasure Island for about two weeks and was tired of living in limbo. I wanted to get on with my career. I wanted to get to sea.

After about an hour, they called me up to the desk and handed me my orders and a check, which was my travel pay. They told me I had six days to report to the Naval Training Center in Great Lakes, Illinois, and it was up to me how I got there. Hooray! At last, I was on my way!

My first stop was the base credit union, where I cashed the check, then back to the barracks to pack up my seabag and check out.

I debated on how I was going to get to Great Lakes. I could either go to the airport and fly there, or—since they gave me six days to get there—I could take the Greyhound bus, which was cheaper, plus I could see the country. Well, the bus won out, so I went to the Greyhound station, bought a ticket to Chicago, and was on my way.

I chose the front seat on the bus so I could see everything. Up until this point, the only parts of the US I had seen were California and Oregon. I was on the adventure of my lifetime, and I wanted to see it all. The bus pulled out and headed east. I was so excited. We crossed over into Nevada, and since it was suppertime, the driver pulled into a diner, shut the bus off, and announced that we had thirty minutes to eat. The driver was the first one off the bus, so he was the first one to get his meal. Fortunately, I was the second since I was in the front seat.

Anyone who has ridden a bus cross-country can tell you, it's not what it's cracked up to be. I rode that bus for three days, had short meals, and couldn't change my clothes. Buses aren't made for sleeping, and the scenery is monotonous. It was absolutely miserable. Time seemed to stand still. After about a day and a half, I regretted my decision. I chalked that one up to experience, as I have since, on my "bright ideas."

*Finally*, after three days, we pulled into Chicago at about four in the morning. I was exhausted, dirty, and hungry. I got off the bus, got my seabag, and made my way to the train station where I had to catch a train to take me the last fifty miles to the navy base. The train ride was unremarkable, other than the fact that it was my first time riding on a train. It took about an hour, and finally, I arrived at the train station in Waukegan, Illinois, which was right outside of the Naval Training Station. I grabbed my seabag and headed for the main gate and was finally there.

I checked in to the admin building, was given a check-in sheet and directions, and started my check-in process. I was tired, dirty, and hungry, and vowed to myself that I'd never do something stupid like that trip again. From then on, I was flying.

My first stop to check in was the barracks. I checked in, and was assigned a room (this was cool, they actually had rooms). I unpacked my seabag into a locker, took a shower (I desperately needed one), put on a clean uniform, and headed out to continue my check-in. Then I was ready.

They had a great mess hall, the food was pretty good, and the barracks was only a block away from the enlisted men's club, right across the street from the gunnery school. I was in heaven.

The Great Lakes Naval Training Center, Service School Command, was a pretty big base. The schools they had there were gunnery school, electronic technician school, boilerman school, engineman school, machinist mate school, fire controlman school, radarman school, and hospital corpsman school.

There were schools and barracks all over the place. I thought the gunnery school was the most impressive. It was a huge, green glass building, and inside was another building in the middle, which was three stories high and contained all the classrooms. All the rest of the building were actual operating weapons systems. There were gun mounts and missile systems everywhere. I didn't know it at the time, but I was to return there two more times, one for an advanced weapons school (class C school) and then for a four-year tour as an instructor.

The barracks was wonderful. There were four men to a room, we had closets instead of lockers, and the bunks were large and comfortable. I never had more than two roommates; it was doable. We stood three-section duty, which meant that every third day, I had to stand a watch and make extra musters, but it wasn't bad. Three-section duty is pretty standard in the navy.

The actual "school" I was to attend was gunnery class A school. That's where you learn the basics of your navy trade, or "rate."

My first two weeks there were spent in "regiment." It was a holding company for sailors who were waiting for their class to start or had completed their training and were waiting on orders for their next command. The navy had to keep us gainfully employed, so they gave us brooms and "swabs" (mops), and that's what we pretty much did all day. Oh yeah, we shoveled snow a lot.

After about two weeks, my class started. There were about thirty of us. These guys were my first "family" in the navy. We were to stay together for sixteen weeks of training. I can still remember all of them to this day. They were a good group of guys.

Since I was an E-3 (or seaman), I was appointed as the assistant class leader. There was another guy, Toby, who was senior to me. I had no idea that becoming a gunner's mate was so complicated. They taught us all about electricity, electronics, hydraulics, motors, explosives, small arms, gun systems, missile systems, you name it. The curriculum was pretty intense, and we had to take a test every Friday on what we had learned that week. There was a lot more to becoming a gunner's mate than just shooting guns.

Liberty in Great Lakes was pretty cool. There was a lot to do on base. They had a skating rink, several enlisted men's clubs, a gymnasium, a movie theater, and a navy exchange. One of the enlisted men's clubs had about twenty pool tables and a ton of pinball machines. I got to be a pretty good pool player. Off base was "The Strip." We were discouraged from going there, but that just made it more attractive for us.

The Strip consisted of several bars, shops, and restaurants that catered to us sailors. It was also a hangout for prostitutes and con men. There was a jewelry store there that featured a "mother's ring," which you could buy at an inflated price and send home to your mother. The salesmen were pretty high-pressure and even offered to sell it to you "on terms." Easy financing. No, I didn't fall for it.

Liberty also consisted of trips into Chicago and up to Milwaukee. I really enjoyed those trips. You had to get there by train, but the train was right next to the base. I really enjoyed Milwaukee because the drinking age in Wisconsin was eighteen.

Even though I was only seventeen, I altered my ID card, so it showed I was eighteen. Nobody ever caught on. I wonder if there's a statute of limitations on something like that. Oh well, what could they do? Send me to prison for falsifying my ID when I was seventeen? It sure was fun though. I can see the headlines now: "70-Year-Old Navy Veteran Gets Prison Term for Falsifying ID at 17!"

Great Lakes is *cold*. I grew up in California and Oregon. I had no idea that any place other than the Arctic could be so cold. I got there in February, and it seemed to stay below freezing until I left in early May. Up until this point, I had never had to shovel snow. I got my fill though.

When the sixteen-week A school was finished, I got to sew my "crossed cannons" onto my uniform. I was so proud of those cannons. We graduated, and they gave us our orders immediately. *Finally*, I was going to sea.

My orders were to a DLG (destroyer, light, guided), which is the navy's way of saying "guided, missile-equipped destroyer" homeported in Pearl Harbor, Hawaii. She was the USS *Reeves*, DLG-24, and she was to be my home for the next three and a half years.

I had packed my seabag the night before, so I was ready. We'd all completed our checkout the day before, so we were ready to go. Three of my classmates and I shared the cab fare to the airport. When we got there, it was pretty sad. We were parting ways, probably never to see each other again. That was my first experience of losing my buddies. We were like a family, had been through so much together, and now we had to part company. I guess you get used to it in the service. I was to have to go through it many more times throughout my naval career. So, when we got to the airport, we said our goodbyes, and all headed off in different directions.

When they gave me my orders, they included thirty days' leave prior to reporting aboard. So I was headed home. I'd only been gone a few months, but I *was* a little homesick.

My leave flew by in the wink of an eye—had fun, got to see my high school friends and my family, but I was pretty excited to get going, and my mind was on what was ahead of me.

Finally, the day came for me to leave. My dad took me to the airport where I caught a plane to San Diego, because that was where I was supposed to catch my ship. One thing I learned in the navy is that ships rarely sit still. I've chased them all over the world, trying to catch up to them.

I landed in San Diego, took a cab to the navy base, checked in, and was told that my ship wasn't there. *Of course.* Why would it be? She was out at sea doing training ops with the rest of the fleet. So . . . I checked into the transit barracks to wait for her to come back in.

Transit barracks *suck*. The only people in transit barracks are guys waiting on their ships to pull in, guys waiting on orders to their next duty station, and guys processing out of the navy. This was back when they had the draft, so not everyone was patriotic and gung ho. There were some pretty malcontent sailors there that were processing out of the navy—some of them because of court marshals and some who had just served out their time.

I learned the first day about how shady a transit barracks can be. I drew my linen, made up my bunk, with my blanket folded at the foot and the pillow at the head, stowed my clothes in my locker, locked it, then headed out to check out the base. I went down to the piers just to see for myself that my ship wasn't there. Then I went to the mess hall for supper. When I got back to the barracks, my blanket and pillow were gone. I went down to the office, which was closed, so I had a terrible night with no blanket and pillow. The next morning when the office opened, I told the petty officer what happened.

He just chuckled at me, handed me another pillow and blanket, and told me, "Kid, let it be a lesson. When you're in a transit barracks, never, ever, under any circumstances, leave anything out and unlocked. It'll be gone in a heartbeat."

Lesson learned.

My stay at the transient barracks lasted about a week. Every morning, we would muster and get our work assignment for the day. It usually consisted of picking up trash on the base or cleaning the barracks. Knock-off was at 1530, and we were allowed to go on liberty. But since I'd been on leave for thirty days, I was broke, so I mostly just wandered around the base.

Finally, after a week, during morning muster, instead of giving me my work assignment, the petty officer told me, "Get your ass over to admin, your ship's pulling in today."

Man, it was actually going to happen. I pretty much ran to the admin building, picked up my orders, then back to the barracks to pack up and check out. I was on my way to my new home.

# CHAPTER TWO

# Kiddie Cruise

A "kiddie cruise" is what sailors refer to when a fellow sailor is underage, as in seventeen. As it turned out, I was the youngest member of the *Reeves's* crew. Everyone thought of me as a kid, but I took it in stride and didn't let it get to me.

When I left the transient barracks, I went straight down to the pier that she was supposed to be berthed at. This was about midmorning. I kept watching the harbor entrance for her, but there was no ship. I sat on that pier all day until finally, about 0330, there she was, coming into the harbor.

She was beautiful, and she was going to be my home for the next few years, for better or for worse. She was a Leahy class DLG, commonly referred to as a "cruiser," but her designation was "destroyer." She was 535 feet long, 53 feet wide at the beam, had terrier missile launchers fore and aft, an antisubmarine rocket launcher forward of the superstructure, two triple-mark 32 torpedo tubes amidships, and two 3"/50 (3-inch/50-caliber) rapid-fire twin gun mounts aft of amidships. Her crew consisted of 413 sailors (32 officers and 381 enlisted).

She was awesome. She was built in 1960, and I found out later in my life that she was decommissioned in 1992, sold to New Zealand, and was used for target practice and sunk off the coast of New Zealand. It makes me sad. She was an awesome ship and was my home for three and a half years.

I watched her glide up to the pier. The crew got the mooring lines over and secured, then a crane set the brow in place, and as soon as the traffic on and off died down, I went aboard.

It happened to be a Friday afternoon, and the ship had been underway about two weeks, so everyone but the duty section headed ashore. I reported to the officer of the deck and gave him my orders. He welcomed me aboard and had the duty master-at-arms come up and take charge of me.

The duty MAA took me down below, issued me my bedding, then took me through the ship to a berthing compartment way forward in the bow. He showed me which rack I was assigned and told me that since it was a weekend, I was free to go on liberty and that I was to muster at the MAA office on Monday morning to start my check-in process. That was it.

I stowed my gear in my locker, made my rack, and then just sat there. The berthing compartment was deserted. Everyone was ashore, and there was nobody to ask about where anything was, like the messdeck. I was lost. After a while, I heard them pass the word for supper over the intercom, so I worked up the nerve to go wandering in search of the messdeck. A navy ship is pretty complicated; it takes a while to learn your way around.

At first, it was like a maze, but I finally found the messdeck, got in line, got my food, sat down by myself (since I didn't know anyone), and ate supper. After supper I found my way up to the main deck and just wandered around, taking it all in. When it got dark, I decided that since I was broke and tired, I'd just go hit my rack, which would also make time pass quicker.

And then it hit me. I had no idea where the berthing compartment was! I had gotten so turned around I couldn't even remember where the messdeck was. Some "first" day aboard my ship! I wandered for what seemed like an hour. I couldn't ask for directions from anyone because I wasn't told the name of the berthing compartment, but eventually, I found it.

The next day I woke up when they passed reveille. I was getting dressed when a guy came into the compartment who happened to have the rack just above mine. He'd been on liberty but had duty that day. He introduced himself to me and was very friendly. I learned from him that we were in supply department berthing and that he was a storekeeper. He was also a seaman, same rank as me. He said that the ship was going to be in port for about a week then head back to its homeport in Hawaii.

He showed me around the ship, which really helped me get oriented, and even sat with me during breakfast, lunch, and supper. His name was Mike, and he turned out to be one of my best friends while I was on board. We even had some adventures together, but that'll come later. It was nice to have someone to talk to and help me find my way. I still think of him from time to time and have even tried to find him, but without success.

The weekend passed (pretty slowly), and eventually, it was Monday morning. I reported to the MAA office, and they contacted my leading petty officer to come and take charge of me. He was a fire controlman first class and treated me well, a pretty nice guy. He took me to the leading gunner's mate to help me get checked in.

The leading gunner's mate was a third class named Dave. Dave was a black guy from Chicago. He was to be my first "mentor" aboard ship. He was my immediate boss and taught me so much. I owe a lot to him. He got me a rack in Second Division, where the rest of the gunner's mates berthed; helped me move my gear out of supply; and took me around to check in.

Checking in on a ship is a lot different than on shore. I had to check in to the sick bay, personnel office, and disbursing. I also had to check in with my leading petty officer, chief petty officer, division officer, department head, executive officer, and finally, the captain. Finally finished with my check-in process, I was ready to start my new life.

I was assigned to gun mount 31, which was on the starboard side of the ship. Mount 32 was on the port side. I worked directly for Dave, who taught me the ropes. My main job was to do maintenance on the gun mount, but in addition to that, I was assigned to clean the berthing compartment and head on a rotating basis with the other seamen in my division.

I also had to do "magazine temperatures," which meant I had to go around every morning and record the temperatures of all the ammunition magazines and ammunition storage lockers. I had to fill out a magazine temperature report that had to be turned in to the officer of the deck before noon. I was pretty busy, and time passed quickly.

After a week, we finally got underway. It was wonderful. I was finally a navy sailor, a member of a ship's crew, and we were headed out to sea. It was everything I'd dreamed about. I was where I wanted to be. It was amazing how quickly I blended in with the rest of the crew and became accustomed to the ship's routine. We were on our way to Hawaii.

My division, Second Division, consisted of about twelve guys—five gunner's mates and seven fire controlmen (FTs for short). Gunner's mates maintain and fire the ship's guns. They also control and maintain all the ship's ammunition, magazines, and complement of small arms. Fire controlmen maintain and operate the gunfire control equipment. I think there is a misconception that the ship's gunners actually aim the guns. The only exception would be if the fire control equipment were knocked out, the guns would be able to aim and fire on their own. The navy does exercise this type of fire control to keep the gun crews able.

We also had two chiefs and a division officer. We were a pretty small division and had our own berthing compartment with about sixteen racks in it. On a navy ship, your division sort of becomes your family. You live together and work together. You become pretty close, like brothers. The rest of the crew are also a sort of family—you're all in the same boat, so to speak.

After about four days of being underway and steaming southwest, the ship scheduled a gun shoot. It was my first. Dave was the mount captain, and he assigned me as a first loader. We did the prefire checks and got the guns ready.

A 3"/50 rapid-fire twin-mount is manned by about twelve guys, a mount captain, two local surface operators, four first loaders, and about five ammunition passers. In addition, the ready service magazine is manned by about eight crewmen, whose job it is to pass the ammo out through passing scuttles to the ammo passers, who then put the rounds into rotary magazines on the back of the gun mount so the first loaders, who are on the gun, can grab them and load them into the gun.

The ship finally went to general quarters, and we manned up. Once we were manned, we got the order to load up. At this point, my adrenaline was probably pumping harder than it ever had before. I was *stoked!* Dave got the order to switch to auto, and the gun mount swung out on the beam and was constantly moving to keep the barrels pointed to the same spot about ten thousand yards out.

Dave got the order to commence fire, and when the first round went off, I almost shit my pants. I thought the world had exploded! I had never in my life heard a noise so loud. I was holding a round on the guides, ready to insert it after the gun indexed, and damn near dropped it.

After that, everything became kind of a blur. I was trying to keep my footing on the moving gun mount and trying to get the rounds out of the rotary magazine and into the gun, all while dynamite seemed to be exploding everywhere. Oh yeah, I didn't mention that since it was an open mount, every time a round went off—which was about every three seconds—all the hot cinders from the burnt powder would blow back on us, stinging our arms and faces.

We fired for about thirty or so rounds, and in no time at all, it was over. We got the order to cease fire then shift back to local, then they passed the word to secure from general quarters. After we stowed the gun mount back in its normal position, everyone left the gun mount except Dave and me. I know that my face had to have been white as a sheet, except for the soot and ash all over me, because Dave just kind of chuckled to himself and shook his head. That was my initiation to naval gunfire. The next time, and the hundreds of subsequent times, I was prepared for it. It was actually fun and exciting, and I fell in love with it. I was glad I made the decision to be a gunner's mate.

The rest of the trip was pretty uneventful. I was getting to know the rest of the crew, and they were getting to know me. I made friends outside my division and was slowly learning everybody's names. The food on the *Reeves* was excellent for the most part, and I was happy and content.

We finally made it to Pearl Harbor, our home port. I was really excited as I stood in ranks with everyone else watching the shoreline pass by. We eventually made it to Bravo piers and moored, then it was time for liberty call.

By this time, I had been paid, so I had money in my pocket. I was ready for some liberty. I was excited to see Hawaii. A couple of guys I'd made friends with invited me on liberty with them; they were going to go down to Waikiki. Of course, I went with them, since I had no idea where anything was or how to get there. I had a blast!

The summer of 1972, the ship pretty much stayed around Hawaii. We'd go out on local ops for sometimes a week, sometimes a few days, but spent a lot of time in port preparing for our upcoming deployment to Vietnam. During this time, I was able to explore a lot of the island, got to know my way around, and spent a lot of time at the beach. I was loving it! I'd go out with my shipmates, drink a lot of beer, and just have fun. I was having the time of my life. I often thought of my high school friends and wondered what they were up to, probably the same old stuff.

Summer passed pretty quickly. I had a few more gun shoots under my belt and felt a lot more confident in my role as a gunner's mate. I was pretty well blended into the crew and was starting to feel pretty "salty."

On September 16, we got underway for our deployment. All the married guys and the guys with girlfriends were looking pretty low, but the rest of us were pumped. The guys that had deployed before told me stories of what to expect, and I was enthralled. This was going to be the absolute greatest adventure of my life. What I didn't realize was that it was going to involve a huge amount of time underway. Up to this point, the longest I had been out to sea was probably two weeks at a stretch. I wasn't prepared for what lay ahead.

After about a week, we pulled into Guam for refueling. What a disappointment that was. We were only there for about four hours, and nobody was allowed to go ashore. From what I learned later in my career, I didn't miss out on much.

We proceeded southwest, day after day. Our next stop was going to be the Philippines, my first foreign port. All the guys who had been there before were getting pretty excited about it. I heard so many stories about it. I was in awe and didn't know what to believe. Sometimes being the new guy, you were told things that weren't true.

We finally made it to the Philippines; the entire crossing took about two weeks. We moored, then it was liberty call! The guys in my division took me with them, since it was my first time there and I needed to be "taught the ropes."

Wow, the stories were true! Subic Bay Naval base was huge. They had everything you could think of for entertaining sailors. There was a golf course, several enlisted clubs, a go-kart track, a navy exchange, a model airplane field—you name it, they had it. But the big attraction was the town just outside the main gate, Olongapo City.

There were money changers on base, just before you walked out of the main gate. We stopped, changed our money to pesos, and headed out the gate into town. There was a river that separated the navy base from the town, so you had to cross a bridge to get to Olongapo. The sailors called it the "Shit River." All the sewage from Olongapo flowed into Shit River, hence its nickname, and the smell was overpowering. That was my welcome to Olongapo. What was sad was that there were little kids in canoes next to the bridge who would call up to the sailors to throw money into the river, and they would dive in to grab the coins before they sank to the bottom.

"Hey, Joe, throw me pesos," I can still hear it in my mind.

The average person in the United States has no idea how well they have it. Nobody I ever knew had to swim in sewage to put food in their stomachs. I wonder, to this day, what kind of diseases those kids came down with and how many survived very long. That was the first of many awful, inhumane things I was to see during my naval career.

After crossing Shit River, the main drag of Olongapo was Magsaysay Drive. It was lined with bars and nightclubs as far as you could see. On every street corner were carts with "barbecue" for sale. It smelled wonderful, but I was warned by the other guys not to eat any of it because it was probably either monkey, cat, or dog meat. Everywhere were little kids begging for money, people selling everything imaginable, and bar girls trying to get sailors to come into their bar. Also, at the time, Olongapo was under martial law, so there were armed guards outside every bar we came to.

We finally got to the bar we were headed for, D' Carrier Club. The guys I was with had been there before, and it was their preferred bar. It was pretty cool. They had a live band that played a lot of Led Zeppelin, cheap drinks, and lots of pretty women. We sat down at a large, round table where served cold San Miguel beers, and we were immediately the main attention of a bunch of pretty women. I was dumbfounded. A lady came up to me, said her name was Rosie, and asked if I'd buy her a drink. Of course I did. She sat with me the entire evening.

I mentioned earlier that Olongapo was under martial law. They had a curfew that was strictly enforced. The streets were "off-limits" from 2300 until 0600. Sailors either had to be back on base by eleven, in a hotel room, or in their girlfriend's home. When it got to be about 2230, the bar started shutting down, and everyone was leaving.

I was getting ready to head back to the base, and Rosie grabbed me by the hand and said, "Come with me."

I took her hand, and she led me out into the street. We got into a "jeepney," and I was lost from there. We eventually got out of the jeepney and walked a few blocks to her home. I'll stop there.

The next morning was crazy. She got me up just before six and took me out to the street and flagged down a "tricycle," a small motorcycle with a sidecar. We got in, she said something to the driver, and away we went. She got me back to the main gate. It only cost me three pesos, which was about fifty cents in US dollars.

I made my way back to my ship, changed into my uniform, ate breakfast (despite the hangover), and made it to quarters. She ended up being my girlfriend for quite a while, at least whenever we were in Subic. What she did the rest of the time, well, I have no idea. Maybe she just waited for me to come back. (Yeah right.)

I loved Subic. I was seventeen—what seventeen-year-old kid wouldn't love it?

We stayed there for about a week. We were getting fitted with something on the ship I can't discuss to this day, then we were on our way to Vietnam. This was in late September, early October of 1972. The US had launched Operation Linebacker in May of that year in response to the Easter offensive that North Vietnam had launched previously that year. We were doing air strikes and bombing runs on the North Vietnamese infrastructure to disrupt their supply line from China. We were bombing railroads, bridges, airfields, roads, and anything else we could find that would deter the NVA from getting supplies. When we arrived, it was in its fifth month.

Vietnam for a sailor on a ship is a little different than in country. You're in a combat zone, but the threat isn't all around you. It's still there, and constant, but not hidden. We did a variety of duties while we were there. We spent a lot of time on Yankee Station, as plane guard for aircraft carriers, which were doing air strikes in support of linebackers. All day and all night, they'd launch and recover planes. We also spent a lot of time on PIRAZ station, which was radar picket duty, and the farthest north of all the stations or areas of operation. We also did search and rescue. We carried an SH-3 Sea King helicopter and the air detachment to maintain it, which we deployed to rescue downed pilots.

More often than not, we were in sight of land except when we were a plane guard for a carrier. The ships deployed to the Gulf of Tonkin during the Vietnam War were affectionately referred to by sailors as the Tonkin Gulf Yacht Club. Don't be mistaken—there was nothing "yacht clubby" about it. It was a dangerous place, and our ships were vulnerable to attack there. In fact, in 1964, the USS *Maddox*, DD-731, was attacked by three NVA torpedo boats, which was one of the things that prompted the US to go to war. A few days later, the USS *Turner Joy* was attacked. There was also the USS *Higbee*, which was attacked by an NVA MIG, which ended up with four wounded and severe damage. Also, the USS *Sterett*, DLG-31, a sister ship of ours, was attacked by two MIGs. She managed to knock one of them out with a Terrier missile.

Lots and lots of underway time. We would stay on "the line" for about a month or more at a time, then would pull into various ports for about three or four days. While we were in the Gulf of Tonkin, we stood condition 3 watches, which meant we manned our weapons 24-7. Watches were four hours on and eight hours off. When we weren't on watch, we were either sleeping or working. The whole time we were there, I never got more than about six hours of straight sleep. One thing about sailors—they can sleep pretty much anywhere, anytime, and can fall asleep almost instantly. You learn to grab it when you can. A ten-minute nap can do wonders.

I have to mention this because it was such a big part of the deployment. The *Reeves*'s desalination plant "sucked." A desalination plant is what makes fresh water for a ship; it converts salt water into fresh water. You need fresh water for the boilers, cooking, showers, and laundry. The priorities for fresh water are also in that same order. Our plant was old and in desperate need of repair. The result was constant "water hours." The plant could only distill so much, and we used most of it up feeding the boilers.

The result was that there was barely enough water left for showers or laundry. We'd go two to three weeks at a time without a shower, and when we *did* get them, they were "navy" showers. Want to know what it's like living with four hundred guys who haven't had a shower or fresh laundry for two or three weeks? Believe me, you don't want to know. I remember going up to the showers when we had enough water for them, and a master-at-arms was there with a stopwatch to time you. We had thirty seconds to get wet (cold water), a minute to soap up, then thirty seconds to rinse off. Water conservation at its finest. We had "water hours" the entire deployment.

The ship's laundry was pretty unreliable. We'd take our laundry bags down on our designated day and "might" get them back in about a week. When they came back, the clothes were usually damp and smelled sour. It was pretty miserable. We'd have to lay them out in the sun all day to get rid of most of the smell. I understood the wisdom then of teaching us in boot camp how to do laundry in a bucket. Rainwater works just fine. About once a month, we'd do "air bedding." We had to strip our racks, then take the mattress topside in the morning to air out, then take them back in late afternoon. I always tied mine down. I remember standing on the fantail one day when we were airing bedding and seeing a mattress go floating by. Someone had to sleep on a hard steel rack after that.

I think the worst part of not having showers was the salt. Out at sea, there's salt everywhere. It's in the air; it's on every surface you touch. If you spend any time topside, it's all over you. Everything forms a thin layer of salt. Without showers, it builds up on your body and *itches*. Then, since it's on your body, it gets transferred to your rack. I can't tell you how many nights I just scratched and scratched. I guess that's why sailors are called "salts."

(One more note on salt. When a navy ship's been at sea and is returning to port, they do a "freshwater washdown." The crew hooks firehoses to the freshwater supply lines and "washes down" the ship. There's salt everywhere, which is highly corrosive to steel, so the entire ship has to be washed down with fresh water. We would start at the highest point of the ship, up in the rigging, and wash it down to the main deck and over the side. The ship could support the use because as soon as we were "pierside," we'd hook up to shore water to refill the freshwater tanks. Washdown starts when you're still out at sea and has to be finished before you get into port. 'Nuff said about that. Not one of my "fondest" memories.)

Gun mount watches sucked. Sitting on a gun mount for four hours straight is "not" fun, especially during the day in the hot sun. And believe me, the sun got *hot* in Vietnam, especially on a steel ship. The only time we were allowed to leave the gun mount was when it rained. There was a compartment next to mount 32 that we used to store our tools and lubricants—that's where we'd take shelter if it rained, and believe me, *it rained*. It would come down in torrents. Sometimes you couldn't see three feet in front of you.

All in all, it wasn't very glamorous. In fact, most of the time it was downright boring, especially when we were a plane guard for the carriers. Our job was to follow the carrier around in case they lost a plane over the side during takeoffs and landings. I never saw it happen, but we were there just in case. There were several stations we were assigned to during our time there. North SAR (or northern search and rescue), mid SAR (or middle search and rescue), and south SAR (or southern search and rescue). We also spent a lot of time on "Yankee Station" and PIRAZ station. No one was any better than the other.

About every four or five days, we'd pull way out away from shore and rendezvous with an oiler to take on fuel. We had to maintain a certain level in case of an emergency. Often, when we would "unrep" (underway replenishment), the oiler would send over mail for us, which was always a high point. I loved it when I would see those orange and red bags come across on the highline. It meant word from home and the outside world. We'd also exchange movies, which meant something new to watch in the evenings.

Life on the line was pretty much the same day after day. There wasn't much time for recreation. Any spare time we got was spent writing letters, reading books, or watching the movie on the messdecks after supper was over and cleanup was finished. The feeling of isolation was incredible.

GIs overseas often referred to home as "back in the world," because that's exactly what it was. Over there we were cut off from "the world." Letters would sometimes take up to a month to "catch up" to us, so any news was a month old, any care packages we got from home were usually beat to shit, and any cookies that wives or mothers sent were always stale and mostly crumbs by the time we'd get them. There was no television, so we had no idea what was going on in the world. We were in our own world over there.

Supplies. That was another issue. Sometimes we'd get food supplies from the oilers. They'd highline them across on cables while the hoses were across and pumping fuel. Sometimes we'd rendezvous with a supply ship, and they'd fly supplies over to us in cargo nets suspended under helicopters and set them on our fantail. We (my division and I) didn't mind these "vertreps" (vertical replenishment). Even though it would take hours and was an "all-hands" evolution, we were okay with it. You see, we had a plan for these.

The crew would form a chain from the flight deck, which was on our fantail, through the passageways of the ship to the ship's storerooms. This chain happened to go right by the hatchway of our berthing compartment. We'd always make sure a couple of us were in that chain right at the hatchway, and one guy would hide down in the berthing compartment. When the supplies started coming down the line, the guys at the hatch would watch to see what it was, and if it was something good (like a case of tuna fish, crackers, potato chips, or dried beef), it would "accidentally" get detoured into our berthing compartment. We always had snacks when we wanted them. We did get caught once. By the captain.

We kept our supply of ill-gotten booty in our laundry locker covered with laundry bags. One day we had a captain's berthing compartment inspection, and he happened to open the laundry locker and move aside a laundry bag, and lo and behold, there was a case of US Navy tuna. We had forgotten to move it elsewhere before the inspection. He was pretty cool about it though. He asked how it got there, and of course, we all played dumb. He just kind of chuckled and told us to get it back to the messdecks.

(Just a sidenote here—you get three square meals a day aboard ship. Breakfast, lunch, and supper. We were also served "midrats" [midnight rations], which wasn't really a meal but a "snack." It was served to the oncoming midwatch and the offgoing eight-to-twelve watch every night underway. It was served between 2330 and 0015 hours and usually consisted of whatever leftovers we had from supper, boiled hotdogs, chicken soup, or whatever was quick and easy for the cooks. The rest of the time, if you got hungry, there was no food available unless you bought cookies and snacks from the ship's store. If you were broke, you were just out of luck.)

I learned a couple of things early on. First, grab an orange, apple, or banana at breakfast, and stash it in your locker for later—you'll be glad you did. Second, make friends with the "night baker." He was the guy who'd get up at 0400 and bake whatever needed baking for the next day. There was nothing worse than waking up at 0330 to stand the rev watch, which went from 0345 to 0745, and smelling cinnamon rolls baking and not being able to have any. My good friend Artie was the night baker. He would always let me into the galley and let me have whatever it was he was baking. My favorite was either donuts or cinnamon rolls. Believe me, the smell would waft through the whole ship.

October was a pretty shitty month. The first thing that happened was the USS *Newport News.* She was a heavy cruiser with 6"/47 gun turrets. She was doing naval gunfire support on October 1 when she had a high explosive round prematurely detonate in the center barrel of her number 2 turret. Twenty sailors lost their lives. We pulled into Subic Bay about a week behind her and tied up just down the pier from her.

I remember walking past her. The gun barrel was still elevated in its last firing position. I think that was the moment when it really hit home for me. It was very sobering. This wasn't just fun and games. Guys were losing their lives, and being a gunner's mate, it made me realize just how dangerous my job was. I guess I grew up that day. I'm so sorry for those guys. I often thought about what would happen if something similar had happened to me.

I've been through dangerous situations on the gun mounts throughout my career, and what consoled me the most was that it would be instantaneous. I probably wouldn't feel a thing. I'd just be gone. So, in those situations, I just carried on and didn't think about it.

I turned eighteen on the seventeenth of October. I'm really not sure where we were. All I know is that we were back on the line. There was no "birthday party," no celebration of any kind, just the same routine as any other day. What was funny though was, a couple months later, probably about February, we had mail call, and I received my "draft notice." I thought that was so funny! I asked my chief what I should do about it. He just laughed and told me to "shitcan it."

I'm not really sure about the timeline, but at some point (I believe it was in October), I was up by mount 31. It was either late morning or early afternoon when the bos'n's mate of the watch came over the loudspeakers:

"This is not a drill, this is not a drill. General quarters, general quarters. All hands man your battle stations. Reason for general quarters, inbound enemy aircraft."

I don't think we'd ever manned up for GQ so fast. I swear, we were manned up within thirty seconds. Dave, I, and Ray (my fellow seaman gunner's mate and best friend) were all at mount 31, so it was just a matter of climbing on the gun, pulling the train and elevation securing pins, and loading up.

Once we got comms with gun control, we shifted into auto and were locked in with the director. We were told that two enemy MIGs were inbound, just above the surface of the water. Combat had picked them up, and the missile fire control was locked on and tracking. Both missile launchers had "birds on the rail," and we were ready to go. I remember scanning the horizon watching for them, my adrenaline pumping overtime. This was the exact same scenario as the USS *Sterett*'s encounter earlier that year, when she shot one down with a terrier missile—same class of ship (Leahy), same area. We were all literally shitting our pants waiting for it.

To this day, I don't know what happened. Maybe they detected our fire control radar locked on them, but they turned and banked away. Talk about relief! That was probably the scariest thing I ever experienced in my life. I admit, I was afraid, but I wasn't so afraid that I wouldn't have done my job; the adrenaline would have taken care of that. We were definitely "in harm's way."

The high point in November was "crossing the line." I don't remember where we were headed, but it was down by the equator. The captain altered course enough so that we would cross it. The navy does a ceremony whenever they cross the equator. Historians have traced it back about four hundred years. When you cross, you become a "shellback"; prior to that, you're a "pollywog." Some sailors never get a chance to cross; some end up crossing multiple times. I ended up being the latter during my career.

At 0600, on the sixteenth of November, all of the pollywogs (guys who'd never crossed before) were rounded up. The uniform of the day for pollywogs was dungarees, inside out and backward, tennis shoes, and our underwear (or skivvies) on over our pants, inside out and backward. We were herded by the shellbacks up to the foc'sle (or bow)—officers, chiefs, enlisted, it didn't matter. On a later ship, I even saw our captain go through it.

Once we were all on the foc'sle, we were ordered to get on our hands and knees. They immediately started spraying us with fire hoses, so we were soaked. We had to crawl on our hands and knees, all the way back to the fantail (or stern), where we had to appear before "King Neptune," who was actually the most senior shellback aboard (regardless of rank), and his royal court, to see if we were worthy of becoming shellbacks. There were probably about three hundred of us pollywogs, so you can imagine how long this all took; it seemed like "forever."

I was wet, cold, hungry (didn't get any breakfast—no pollywog did), and tired. The whole time we were crawling along the main deck, we had shellbacks with three-foot-long pieces of firehose (called shelalees) beating our wet asses. When I finally made it to the fantail, and King Neptune's court, I was called before him, where he sentenced me for my crime of being a "pollywog."

My punishment was to kiss the royal baby's belly (which was covered in a thick layer of black grease); kiss the royal princess's foot (which was covered in the same grease); lie in the "coffin" (which was a large wooden box where they made us swallow raw eggs); crawl through the "garbage chute" (which was a canvas tube about three feet wide and twenty feet long and filled with about a week's worth of food scraps from the messdecks); and finally, go through the dunking tank. They make you get in, then submerge your head, bring you back up, ask you what you are, and if you say "pollywog," they dunk you back down and repeat it, again and again, until you say, "I'm a shellback."

It only took twice for me. I catch on pretty fast. I was a mess. All of us were. But in retrospect, it was fun and will live in my memory till the day I die. The only thing comparable to it was my chief's initiation, which I'm not at liberty to discuss. If you're an old chief, you know; if not, you'll never know.

So, there I was, my first year in the navy, and I was already a Vietnam vet and a shellback. By the way, it took me forever to get myself cleaned up, and when we finally got to eat, I don't remember eating so much. I think we had steak for supper that afternoon. A hell of a day.

Back on the line again for more of the same. Back to gun mount watches and routine. The weather was getting a little bit rough. Normally, the *Reeves* had a pretty slow pitch and roll. It was comfortable; it would kind of rock you to sleep at night. Later in my career, I was stationed on Knox-class destroyers, which were a lot more rough riding.

The *Reeves*, though, was pretty gentle and soothing. During late November and early December, it got pretty rough. The waves would come up over the side, and it was almost impossible to work on the main deck. I remember one night. I was lying on my rack trying to sleep. The ship was taking some pretty heavy rolls, and I literally got tossed out of my rack. I hit the deck across the compartment. I wasn't hurt, but it shook the hell out of me. After that, I learned to sleep on my stomach. You're more stable that way, and it's harder to roll out. During this period, gun mount watches were a bitch. With water coming over the side, we had to take shelter in the gun shop almost all the time.

One night I was on the midwatch. It was darker than hell, and the ship was rolling and pitching harder than usual. We were sheltered in the gun shop with one man on the sound-powered phones, so we kept constant communication with gun control, and I had to go to the bathroom. We shut the lights off so I could get out (no white lights are allowed at night). I got out and closed the hatch behind me and quickly made my way to the hatch to go inside to the head, except I didn't make it. The ship took a heavy roll, and I slipped on the wet deck, fell, and was quickly sliding toward the outer side of the ship.

I would've gone over the side, except my legs straddled the bottom lifeline. So, there I was, legs dangling over the side, waiting for the ship to roll the other way so I could get up. It finally did, and I was able to get up and find something to hold on to. It scared the holy crap out of me. After that, I always held on to whatever I could reach when I was on the main deck during heavy seas.

On December 18, the US started Operation Linebacker II. This was an effort by Nixon to get the North Vietnamese back to the negotiation table for a ceasefire and to get us out of the war. US Air Forces started bombing the shit out of Hanoi. I'm not really sure where we were at the time; we sailors on the decks were pretty much kept in the dark about the "big picture."

What I *do* remember was that it was getting close to Christmas, but it wasn't like any Christmases I remembered. They set up a fake tree on the messdecks and played Christmas music over the ship's speaker system. I hated it. All it did was remind me of where I was and made me homesick. By the way, the only day we didn't bomb Hanoi was on Christmas Day. Do you know how sailors celebrate Christmas on a ship? They get a turkey dinner.

(Just a side story. Years later, about 2010, I met a guy through a neighbor. He was a Vietnam vet and had served as an armored personnel carrier driver in country. We were at my neighbor's house having a few beers and talking about Vietnam, and he said to me, "Oh, you're one of those REMFs." I asked him what a REMF was, and he said, "Oh, one of those rear echelon motherfuckers." I put down my beer, excused myself, and left, never to return. He had no idea what my Vietnam was like, just as I had no idea about his. But I do know this: we all paid a price, some more than others, but we all paid. If you're a veteran, don't belittle another vet's contribution.)

For some reason, maybe it was just our rotation, but we pulled off the line just before Christmas, even though Linebacker II was in full swing, and headed for Hong Kong. It was my second foreign liberty port and was a welcome break from Vietnam. I did a lot of sightseeing and ate so much food I was almost sick. The clubs were a little expensive, but all our wallets were fat. Being in a combat zone, we got combat pay, and our pay wasn't taxed, so that meant we had more money. Besides, where were you going to spend money at sea?

I got my first tattoo in Hong Kong by a tattoo artist named Pinky Lee. Every sailor had to get a tattoo—or that's what I was told. I've seen some doozies. I knew a machinist's mate that had twin screws (propellors) on his butt cheeks. I once knew a guy that got his penis barber poled. Another guy had the words "Your Name" tattooed on the head of his penis. I knew a first-class hospital corpsman who had a full body suit. The only parts of his body that weren't tattooed were his hands and head. I've seen every kind of dragon, ship, naked woman, lion, tiger, you name it.

My first one was a Chinese dragon. On the Vietnam Campaign Medal, there's a dragon standing behind stalks of bamboo. I was told that it represented the Viet Cong hiding in the jungle. I don't know if that was true, but I got that dragon tattooed on my right shoulder. Many, many years later, my oldest daughter had it tattooed on her ankle in honor of my service over there.

* * *

A little sea story here. There were two or three guys in my division that had gotten in trouble, got sent to captain's mast, and were awarded restriction to the ship. They weren't allowed ashore. They took up a collection among themselves and asked me if I could bring some booze back for them when I went ashore. I agreed. They gave me the money, and I asked them how many bottles they wanted, and when they responded with, "Two or three cases," I almost shit my pants.

Firstly, we were anchored out in the middle of the harbor, and I'd have to take a liberty boat back and forth. Secondly, how in the hell was I going to sneak two cases of booze across the quarterdeck without getting caught? On navy ships, any packages coming aboard get searched by the quarterdeck watch, and alcohol is absolutely illegal aboard ship.

So I went on liberty fretting about how I was going to pull it off. I eventually finished my liberty and headed back to the ship. As I walked along the busy streets, I came to a shop that sold liquor. I went in and found two cases of scotch, and the cases were enormous. Then I got an idea. This was Christmastime. What if I had the store owner wrap them up like presents? It might just work. I paid for the booze and headed for the boat landing carrying two heavy cases of scotch. When we finally got to the ship, I carried them up the accommodation ladder and onto the quarterdeck. *Of course*, the officer of the deck asked me what was in the packages, and *of course*, I was sweating it.

I just smiled at him and said, "Oh, these are just some Christmas presents I picked up for my mom and dad."

He just told me, "Okay, just checking," and away I went.

I was home free. (If you're reading this, OOD from long ago, *gotcha!*)

We had scotch for a long time. To this day, I can't stand it. We'd take a can of Coke or Seven-Up, drink it down a little way, then fill it back up with scotch. We could even walk around the ship with it, and nobody suspected it (as far as I know). Scotch doesn't mix well with anything that I know of. It did the job though.

* * *

After Hong Kong, it was back to the line and back to the same routine. We celebrated the New Year somewhere in the Tonkin Gulf (I'm not sure, it all blended together). We *did* celebrate it with warm scotch though.

On January 27, 1973, Nixon signed the long-awaited ceasefire with North and South Vietnam. I remember that day so clearly.

The captain came over the 1MC (ship's loudspeaker) and announced the news to the crew. Everyone started cheering and yelling—we were pretty happy. We all speculated what was going to happen. Were we going home? Were we going to stand down from condition 3? We speculated on all kinds of things. Rumors started flying around the ship like crazy!

I had a chief once who had a saying, "If you haven't heard a good rumor by noon, start one." That was pretty much what they were—just rumors.

When they announced the ceasefire, the *Reeves* just happened to be the northernmost ship in the Gulf of Tonkin. We were up at North SAR and happened to be the ship that was most in "harm's way." As it turned out, we still stood gun mount watches. We didn't go home early; nothing really changed. And come to find out—the US was the only one to honor the ceasefire; the North Vietnamese just waited until we pulled everyone out.

January gave way to February, and it was just more of the same routine: gun mount watches; gun mount prefires every morning (an extensive check sheet of all the preoperational checks that had to be performed prior to firing; it had to be turned into the captain every morning); and a lot of boredom. We still had to do routine maintenance to the gun mounts—they had to be operational at any given time. Occasionally, we'd do a firing exercise to keep us sharp and the guns limbered up. I always enjoyed those. Every once in a while, we'd talk our division officer into getting us permission to do a "fan fire" with the ship's small arms (of which the gunner's mates were in charge). We'd bring up a bunch of M-14s, .45s, BARs, shotguns, and .30-caliber machine guns and throw soda cans, garbage, five-gallon cans, and whatever we could find over the side to have a target to shoot at. We burned up thousands of rounds, but it was fun.

We occasionally had more port visits during our deployment and had the chance to get off the ship for a couple days. We stopped in Singapore, Japan, Taiwan, and *of course*, Subic Bay. They were all wonderful, and it was always great to get off the ship, have a few beers, and explore.

I mentioned Dave before. He was my immediate supervisor and an awesome mentor for me. I looked up to him like a big brother. He was probably in his early twenties. This was his second or third deployment, and he knew the ropes pretty well. He was a gunner's mate third class.

One day he and I were on mount 32 dropping the breech blocks, a maintenance procedure we had to do once a month and took about three hours per barrel. I was on the gun and looked up at the 01 level, and there, perched on the handrail, was an owl. He was about twelve inches tall and just sitting there.

I said, "Hey, Dave, look, an owl!"

He looked and just said, "So what? Get back to work."

Still being a kid, I got it into my head to "catch" that owl. I started to climb down off the gun mount, and Dave said, "Leave the fucking owl alone, and get back to work!"

I was adamant though about catching that "fucking" owl and continued on my way up to the 01 level to catch it.

As I made my way up there, Dave said, "Okay, you've got two hours' extra duty in the fireroom!"

I thought he was just kidding me, so I kept going. By the time I got to the owl, I had six hours' extra duty, according to Dave. I finally made it to the owl, and not only did the owl tear me a new asshole and fly away, but I also had six hours' extra duty in the fireroom that I worked off two hours every evening after supper. After that, I listened to what Dave said, followed his orders, and never again attempted to "catch" any wildlife that happened to land on the ship.

* * *

Just a side story here. Dave left the ship after we returned from our deployment. He'd gotten orders to shore duty in the Philippines. I figured I'd never see him again. However, on my second deployment on the *Reeves*, I was a petty officer second class. We pulled into Subic Bay on my duty day, and I was assigned shore patrol duty. At about 1800, I reported to the shore patrol headquarters on base, checked in, and was waiting along with everyone else for my assigned beat. I was looking around the room and whom did I see? Dave. He was a petty officer first class, and he was assigned as a permanent military policeman. We called them "hard hats" because they wore white military helmets.

I walked up to him and said, "Hi, Dave."

He couldn't believe his eyes. We hugged and shook hands; it was like meeting up with a long-lost brother.

After the initial greetings were over, he said, "You're coming with me." He went up to the desk, said something to the petty officer, came back to me, and said, "Let's go."

I followed him out the door, and we walked up to a shore patrol van.

He said, "This is my ride. You're going to ride with me tonight."

We got into the van, he drove out the main gate, and I spent the evening riding around with Dave, catching up on old times and enjoying his company. It was pretty neat. Not only did I not have to walk a beat, but I got to spend time with a good friend. The night was also pretty interesting.

Whenever there was trouble at a bar, we'd show up, and Dave would take over. We took a few sailors back to the base that night. Dave invited me to his "crib" the next day. He met me at the main gate and took me to his house. It was pretty nice. He had a maid and a girlfriend, and his house was pretty impressive by Filipino standards. We ended up going out on the town and having a great time. This was in the seventies, and Dave was a black guy, so we went to some black bars.

I was the only white guy there and felt a little uncomfortable, and I guess Dave noticed and told me, "Just chill, Kenny, you're with me. Just enjoy yourself."

I did. It was a liberty that I'll always remember. I had a great time and got to spend time with Dave, whom I considered my navy brother.

* * *

February turned into March, and it was still the same old thing. I was starting to get tired of being at sea, looking at the same horizon day after day, eating the same meals, standing the same watches, and doing the same maintenance over and over. This was what I wanted—this was what I got. We still did unreps, we still did fire drills, we still did flight quarters to launch and recover our helo, we still did supply vertreps—it just seemed to go on and on. The only high points were pulling into new ports, mail call, and knowing that our time there was slowly coming to an end.

One night, after the movie on the messdecks was over, a small group of my friends and I wandered back to the fantail to have a smoke before hitting our racks. I believe we were on the northern SAR station, just off North Vietnam. It was pitch-black. You couldn't see your hand in front of your face. We were standing in a small group, talking about the movie and joking around. All of a sudden, the night erupted into brilliant white light, and there, off our port quarter, probably a hundred feet away, was a ship. They had their searchlights on us. We ran over to the aft lookout and asked him if the bridge knew about it. He told us it was a Russian gunboat that had been following us for a while and were trying to harass us. I could only imagine how busy it was up on the bridge and in CIC (Combat Information Center).

In March of 1973, we'd been in the Tonkin Gulf for about six months. The North Vietnamese released our POWs, and things were looking up as far as the war being over. Everybody was getting excited about "going home." We left Vietnam, made a last stop in Subic, and "headed home." We were going back to "the world."

When you're homeward bound, everyone on the ship is in a good mood. Everyone is happy, and there's just a celebratory spirit in the air. We'd stood down from condition 3, and it was just such a relaxed atmosphere; it's hard to describe. On the last night, before pulling back into Pearl Harbor, I don't think "anyone" slept.

On March 17, 1973, the *Reeves* steamed into Pearl Harbor. The pier was filled with people, mostly wives and girlfriends; it was a wonderful thing to see. I had completed my first of many deployments and felt very proud of myself. I was a "salt." On the other hand, seeing all the wives, girlfriends, and families greeting my shipmates made me feel somewhat lonely and homesick for *my* family. There was no one on that pier for me.

After we got back from Vietnam, I took thirty days' leave to go home and visit my family. I always traveled in my uniform because I was proud of it. I flew into San Francisco airport, got off the plane, and was walking through the airport to the baggage claim. Then this young girl, about seventeen or eighteen, approached me, spit at me, and called me a "baby killer." It caught me completely off guard. I never killed anyone, much less a baby. Then it sank in with me that this was my welcome home. After spending seven months in Vietnam, enduring the heat and rain, the isolation, the long months at sea, the sleepless nights, and the constant threat of attack, this was my thank-you. It still leaves a bad taste in my mouth after all these years.

To add to that, I was eighteen years old, had served in Vietnam, and had been all over the Pacific Ocean, but when my dad and I went to a local bar in Manteca, California, while I was on leave, just to have a beer with my dad, they refused to serve me because I wasn't old enough. I was old enough to go fight for my country, but I wasn't old enough to have a beer with my dad. I just don't get the age thing. At the age of eighteen, you can go to war for your country, be trusted with deadly weapons, but you can't be trusted with a beer. Something here doesn't make a lot of sense and really stinks.

# Three Frigates

After our return from deployment, we settled into our homeport routine. We had a thirty-day stand-down, where we didn't leave port, to give the crew a much-needed break and allow everyone some time to be with their families. After that it was just local ops that would only last a few days at a time, then it was back in port.

I spent my off-duty time exploring Oahu and having fun. I even ended up sharing an apartment off base with a couple of my shipmates. Good times. The ship ended up going into the shipyards late in 1973, then there was no more underway time, just work.

I ended up going home on leave in December of that year for thirty days. I met up with a girlfriend from high school, and all of a sudden, I found myself married. I took her back to Hawaii with me, and life was good. During this same time, I advanced in rank to petty officer third class (E-4) and was eligible for base housing.

After the shipyards, the *Reeves* made another deployment. This one was a lot different than the first in that it was more of a "show the flag" cruise. We made a big circle of the Indian Ocean, along the coast of Africa and along the southern shores of Pakistan and India. I'll talk more about it later. This was also my first deployment as a married man. I also had a newborn daughter who was born just before we deployed. Having a family back in Hawaii seemed to make the deployment go slower than my first one.

It was during this deployment that two things happened to me. The first was that I made petty officer second class; the second was that my enlistment was almost up. I had to either get out of the navy or reenlist. Of course, I reenlisted. I ended up reenlisting for a class C school. It's an advanced school for enlisted men who want to earn an enlisted classification code. In my case, I chose a classification that would allow me to work on 5"/54 gun mounts. The *Reeves* had three-inch guns; I wanted to work on the bigger five-inch guns. A lot more firepower.

My orders came in, and I left the *Reeves* during our last port visit to the Philippines. I had the pleasure of flying back to Hawaii in a C-130 cargo plane; they're lots of fun and very comfortable for passengers. The flight attendants were very attentive to us; they even gave us wax earplugs for the pressure in our ears. Oh yeah, they even treated us to a stale box lunch for our dining pleasure.

The school was in Great Lakes and lasted thirty-two weeks, but by the end of the course, I knew the five-inch guns inside and out. All I can say about the school I attended was that it was "thorough." The gun was a lot more sophisticated than the three-inch I'd been on. I loved the five-inch guns.

After I graduated, I got orders to a "frigate." It was a Knox-class destroyer. She was homeported out of San Diego, which would be a real change for me from Hawaii. She was the USS *Meyerkord*, FF-1058. She was a lot smaller than the *Reeves*, with a length of 438 feet and a beam of 46 feet. The crew consisted of 13 officers and 211 enlisted men.

According to my orders, I was to proceed to San Diego to report aboard. Unbeknownst to me, when I got there, my new ship wasn't. Come to find out, she was on deployment and wasn't due back for another two months. So back to the transient barracks *again*.

This time the transient barracks were full. They didn't have room for me, so they transferred me over to Coronado Amphibious base. I liked it there a lot better than on Thirty-Second Street Naval Base. The transient barracks were pretty empty, and the food in the mess hall was a lot better. Coronado is where they train Navy SEALs. I saw them running with their inflatable boats all the time. I was actually pretty impressed.

The two months in transient was actually a blessing for me. It gave me time to find a house for my wife and daughter and get them moved down there.

Eventually, the *Meyerkord* pulled back in from deployment. When she did, I was on the pier waiting with my orders in hand. There was the usual crowd of people there—wives, girlfriends, kids, and parents. After all the excitement was over and they passed liberty call, I went on board to check in.

By this time in my career, I was pretty used to the check-in routine and learned my way around the ship pretty fast. Since it was a smaller crew, it didn't take long to get to know the rest of the crew. This time I was a petty officer second class and not a green "boot camp," so I was treated a little differently.

After a month and the postdeployment stand-down, the ship started doing local ops again. Five days out, seven days in, another three days out, maybe a week back in. Rarely does a ship just sit pierside for more than a couple weeks at a time.

I was getting pretty well integrated into the crew and was getting more and more comfortable. Being a gunner's mate second class, they assigned me as the mount captain, which was an honor and was very exciting.

As I said before, I loved the five-inch gun. It was a lot more powerful and versatile than the three-inch guns I'd been on. The three-inch guns were "open" mounts, but the five-inch ones were enclosed in a fiberglass dome that protected them from the weather and was somewhat of a shield for shrapnel. The gun only had one barrel, but the rate of fire was about thirty-six rounds per minute.

The entire gun system started in the magazine, two decks down from the main deck. There were two loader drums in the magazine, where the ammunition was loaded. The rounds went up a hoist that then loaded them into a "carrier" in the compartment above the magazine. The carrier took the rounds to whatever position the gun was trained on and transferred the rounds into two more hoists, which then transferred them up into "cradles" (two big mechanical arms that would swing up to wherever the slide was positioned and load the rounds into the gun). All this was automatic and happened in seconds.

All this was controlled by the "mount captain," who operated the control console that was located in the "carrier room." The actual gun was only manned by three people—one of them a junior officer who was the "check sight observer." His job was to make sure the gun wasn't pointing somewhere it shouldn't be when we fired. The other two guys in the mount were stationed on each side of the gun to make sure nothing went wrong and also to give bore reports to the mount captain after a firing run.

Everyone had coms with each other via sound-powered phones.

One of the big differences between the three-inch and the five-inch guns was their "mission." The three-inch guns were for close-range surface and air targets, and the five-inch ones were for long-range surface and air targets, *and* naval gunfire support, or "shore bombardment"

I loved it when we'd go to the NGFS range on San Clemente Island. It was pretty much an all-day thing, and we'd end up firing ninety to a hundred rounds throughout the day—sometimes more, sometimes less. It was exciting and fun. I never got to watch the rounds explode on shore though. I was always on the mount captain's panel in the carrier room and was pretty busy. I can tell you this though, when a five-inch gun fires, it's a hell of a boom, and the whole ship shudders. During rapid-fire salvos, it shudders a lot. A lot of dust falls out of the overhead. We gunners did our part to help keep the ship dust-free.

The ship's bos'n's mates hated it whenever we'd do a gun shoot. Whenever the gun would fire, the empty shell casing would eject out of the front of the gun, hit the deck, and leave half-moon divots in the paint and nonskid. After we were done, they'd have to get paint primer on the divots before the salt water could get a hold on the bare metal and cause rust. If we were doing shore bombardment, there could be a hundred or more divots to paint. On one of my ships, the chief bos'n's mate got smart and ordered some huge mats made out of rope. It actually worked pretty well and reduced the number of divots in the deck.

I was only to spend about two years on the *Meyerkord*, and I never had the opportunity to deploy with her. Our time together was spent doing local ops around the Southern California area. After about a year and a half aboard, she was scheduled for a shipyard overhaul, which happened to be in Portland, Oregon. Sadly, my last few months on board were spent in "dry dock."

In December of 1977, I had reached my sea-shore rotation date. For gunner's mates, it was six years at sea, then four years ashore. There aren't a lot of shore duty billets for gunner's mates. The choices are either recruiting duty, general duty, pushing boots, or a training command. I ended up with orders to (of all places) Great Lakes, Illinois, the US Naval Training Command—particularly, gunnery A school.

I'm not going to go into a lot of detail about it because this is supposed to be about destroyers at sea, but I will say that I enjoyed teaching gun school, and I enjoyed being a "mentor" to so many young sailors. I can say that at one time, I probably knew just about every eighteen- or nineteen-year-old gunner's mate in the entire US Navy. I spent four years there, picked up petty officer first class, and earned another enlisted classification code (instructor, 9502) (my first, 5"/54 technician, was 0876). But I was ready to go back to sea.

After four years ashore, the navy gave me orders to another Knox-class frigate—the USS *Ouellett*, FF-1077. She was homeported out of Pearl Harbor, Hawaii, and I remembered her. When I was on the *Reeves*, we operated with her quite a bit.

So, another move (I had two beautiful daughters by this time), and it was back to Hawaii. My wife and I were pretty excited about it because it was like going home. As I've said before, "Ships rarely sit still."

This time around, the *Ouellett* was deployed overseas but had just recently left, so the navy sent me to her. Anyone who's had to chase a ship to catch up to it can tell you just what kind of a bitch it can be.

I caught a civilian airline from San Francisco that flew first to Seattle, then to Anchorage, Alaska, then out to Hawaii. Then I had to make it to Hickam Air Force Base and catch a transport plane to the Philippines. I landed at Clark Air Force Base, then took a bus to Subic Bay Naval Station. No *Ouellett*. I had missed her. She was on her way to the Indian Ocean.

I checked into the transient barracks *again* and waited for admin to find out where the *Ouellett* was headed. After about a week, I got word, and they gave me orders to proceed back to Clark AFB to catch another flight.

When I checked in at Clark, I had to wait for about six hours for my flight. They finally boarded us (a C-140 transport), and we pulled away from the terminal, sat on the runway for what seemed like forever, then taxied back to the terminal. The pilot came over the intercom and told us that they were having some electrical system problems. We went back into the terminal and waited. After about four hours, they boarded us again. We taxied out to the runway, sat there for about half an hour, then it was back to the terminal for another couple of hours.

The third time we got to the runway, the engines cycled up, and we were off. A few minutes later, the pilot came over the speakers and told us that they still had the electrical problem but that we shouldn't be worried— "It was just to the navigation system"—and that we were going to proceed to our destination, which happened to be Diego Garcia, a tiny little island about two or three thousand miles west of Australia and in the middle of absolutely nowhere! I often wondered how those pilots were able to find Diego Garcia without a navigation system. But they did. That was to have been the longest journey I ever made in my life. It was my career record.

Diego Garcia is a tiny little island out in the middle of the Indian Ocean. It's probably about a quarter mile wide at its widest point. It's shaped like a horseshoe and is about three miles long. There's a harbor entrance about a quarter mile wide on its southern side, if I remember right. The navy ships anchor out in the harbor and use small boats to get back and forth to shore. The island is a British possession, and they lease it to the US for a navy and air force base. It seemed odd to me that when we landed, I had to clear British customs.

There was not much there. There was a landing strip, and there was somewhat of a navy base—which consisted of barracks, a mess hall, a small navy exchange, a package store, an enlisted men's club, officers' club, acey-deucey club, and a chiefs' club. You may have guessed what the popular pastime was on Diego Garcia.

I caught a shuttle van from the airfield to the navy base, went down to the boat landing, found the *Ouelletts* motor whaleboat, boarded, and off we went to my new ship. I was worn out, hungry, and so happy to finally get there.

When I got on board, I was greeted by the officer of the deck, who took my orders then had the petty officer of the watch page one of the gunner's mates. It turned out to be another gunner's mate first class named Mike. I was a little confused because usually ships only had one gunner's mate first class. He took me below and helped me find an open rack. I unpacked, changed into dungarees, went to chow, then hit my rack till the next morning. I was tired.

It didn't take me long to adjust to the crew and the routine. I've always been one to make friends quickly. The *Ouellett* was just like the *Meyerkord*. They were the same class of ship, but there are always differences. The food was good, except for the one cook that didn't know how to fry eggs.

The five-inch gun mount was in decent shape. It needed a little more TLC than it'd been getting, but not in terrible shape. Even though the ship already had a gunner's mate first class, they gave me the gun mount. I kind of figured out later why. My gun crew were a good bunch of guys; they just needed a little more direction than they'd been getting. But in no time at all, we were looking pretty good and getting better. We didn't have a chief gunner's mate at the time, so I was the "go-to" gunner's mate for the gun mount. If there was a breakdown, it was up to me to get it fixed and give an honest assessment to the chain of command.

On this deployment, we operated a lot in the northern part of the Indian Ocean and along the coast of Africa. It was a lot different than Vietnam. We made port visits to Somalia, Pakistan, the western coast of Australia, and of course, a couple back to Diego Garcia. There were some long stretches in between port visits. It was also a long time before we made it back to the Philippines again.

* * *

I have to tell a story here about our visit to Somalia. When we pulled into Djibouti, we weren't allowed liberty. Apparently, the ship was there to help out the Somali government (whatever that was). It seemed that the Somalis were in possession of a captured Russian torpedo boat, and they needed help in getting it running. Our captain offered to help them fix it. I believe we were there for about three days while our machinist mates worked on it.

Anyway, the *Ouellet*'s crew were allowed to leave the ship to go aboard and tour the torpedo boat. The only stipulation was that we had to go in our dress uniforms (whites, of course). Myself and a buddy of mine, another first class, took the opportunity and went aboard. I took my camera and took a lot of pictures. When we were done, we walked up the pier to get over to where the ship was tied.

At the head of the pier was a guard shack. It was like something you'd see in a movie. It was about four feet wide and four feet deep, and it was painted with red and yellow diagonal stripes. In the doorway stood a Somali soldier. He was dressed in khaki shorts and shirt, wore a red beret, and was armed with a Russian Kalashnikov machine gun. It was a perfect picture.

We walked up to within about twenty feet of him, and as soon as I brought my camera up to my face, he went ballistic. He charged his machine gun, pointed it at us with his finger on the trigger, and started screaming at us in Somali. I have no idea what he was saying, but the message came through crystal clear. I took my camera away from my face, and we put our hands in the air and started backing away, all the time saying, "Okay, it's cool, don't shoot."

He continued aiming at us and yelling, but we just kept backing away. After we were about fifty or sixty feet away from him, he finally lowered his gun but kept yelling at us until we were probably fifty yards from him. I think I pissed him off a little. Was I scared? You better believe it. Did I shit my pants? Almost. Did we go ashore again? Not on your life.

We visited Somalia again later in the deployment and actually got to go ashore on liberty. The second time was in Berbera. One of the first things I saw was open-sided warehouses filled with bags of wheat or corn, not sure which, but they were all labeled "Care." When I got out into "town," it was a bunch of mud huts and not really a town at all. Everywhere you looked, you saw starving people. I'm not sure who got the "Care" sacks, but I'm pretty sure it wasn't the people in town. I can honestly say, Somalia was a *shithole*. The government was corrupt, the place was desolate, and I honestly didn't see that it had anything going for it.

*   *   *

The only high point about our visit to Berbera was that the ship hired a couple vans; loaded up a bunch of beer, food, and our barbecue pits; and had a ship's party at a local beach. The beach was wonderful. The water was crystal clear and warm. My buddy and I went snorkeling out into the ocean; it was beautiful. My buddy got tired and went back, but I wanted to keep going. I was about a hundred yards from shore where the bottom dropped off to about fifty feet. You could see just about forever.

That's when I saw *the shark*. I was all alone, and this thing was maybe fifty yards away from me. It was eight or nine feet long and slowly swimming toward me. Yes, I made a hasty retreat back toward shore. I swam as fast as I could, and every few feet, I'd look behind me. It seemed to take forever to get back to the beach. When I got back to where the water was only three or four feet deep, and the swirling sand made visibility underwater impossible, that's when I worried the most. I never went back into that water. I drank beer and ate food instead. That was enough of an underwater adventure for me.

We made a port visit to Karachi, Pakistan. My first impression wasn't very good when we passed a dead camel floating in the water just outside the harbor. Then there were the flies. We were probably still a mile out when they started swarming the ship. It probably took two weeks after leaving for them to finally disappear. Karachi itself was no treat either. It stank. There were people living in the streets, and some were dying, probably mainly from starvation or disease. There was traffic everywhere, and mixed in with the cars and trucks, there were camels pulling wagons and holding up the traffic.

Alcohol was hard to find. The only ways you could get a beer was either at the US Embassy or trust a taxi driver to take you to some hole-in-the-wall, out-of-the-way place that was populated by some pretty untrustworthy local guys. Not a place to go to by yourself. We always went in groups of three or four.

I remember three or four of us hired a taxi to take us around town sightseeing. The driver spoke very little English but was nice enough. I had to use the bathroom, so I asked the driver if he could find one for us. It took a little bit, but we finally got him to understand.

He pulled over next to a large empty field and said, "Okay?"

"No, no," we said. "We need a toilet."

He said, "Yes, toilet, there," as he pointed at the field.

As we looked at the field, an old woman walked out from behind a wall, lifted up her dress, squatted, and well, did her thing. When she was done and left, I got out, walked out into the field to "go," and it was shocking. There was human shit everywhere. After that, if we had to go, we'd have him take us to the embassy.

While we were out sightseeing, I ran out of film for my camera. I asked the taxi driver if he knew where we could get some. He drove a little bit then pulled over in front of a little shop. I got out of the taxi, walked up to the door, and there, standing next to the door, was a little girl, maybe eight years old. She was dressed in rags and looked like a little skeleton. She was just skin and bones. In her arms was a tiny little baby covered with a ragged little blanket. The baby couldn't have been more than four months old. I looked at that poor little thing, and it was a little skeleton too, just skin and bones, like the little girl.

The little girl held the baby's hand out to me, begging. It broke my heart. I reached into my pocket and pulled out my money and gave that little girl a big wad of rupees. Her face lit up, and I couldn't understand what she was saying in Pakistani. It sounded happy, and she had the biggest smile on her face and tears in her eyes. I had some tears in mine too. I'm so thankful that my daughters never had to experience what that little girl did.

I've thought about that little girl and baby a lot over the years. I hope the money I gave her put some food in their bellies and brought them at least "some" comfort and happiness. I see homeless people every day, holding signs explaining their situation and looking for handouts. They all look pretty well fed to me; often I'll see a fast-food drink next to them. When

I see them, I think back so many years ago about that little girl. This is America, folks, the opportunity is out there. All you have to do is seek it out and work for it. Karachi was *interesting*, to say the least.

There's one thing I can say about operating in the Indian Ocean and the Middle East. *It's hot.* We spent a lot of time underway, and it was always "hot." Being on a steel ship made it even hotter. The sun's glare off the ocean didn't help much either. At least when I was in Vietnam, we'd get rain once in a while. Also, on this deployment, we weren't operating with a bunch of other ships. Supplies and mail were few and far between. Also, when you're in a task force, ships exchange movies back and forth. We didn't have very many ships to exchange "with." We ended up watching a lot of reruns on the messdecks.

When the deployment was finally over, it was back to Pearl Harbor and our families. We got the standard thirty-day standdown, then it was back to the usual local ops and just being part of a destroyer squadron. A week out, two weeks in, three days out, four days in, and on and on it went.

It was during this time that a wonderful thing happened to me. I made chief petty officer! It'd always been my dream to someday become a *chief*, and it finally happened. I can't find the words to describe what it felt like.

For those who don't know, the navy is the only branch of service that has a distinction between an E-6 and an E-7. The purpose of a chief is to be a leader and mentor for his subordinates, and the same for those above him, especially his junior officers. He's a seasoned adviser for both ends of the chain of command. It's a very honored position. When you make chief, you put away your enlisted uniforms and don new "khakis," or officer uniforms. You no longer berth with the enlisted men but in the chief's quarters.

When you're selected for chief, several things happen. First, you're integrated into a "brotherhood" of chief petty officers. During this process, you go through a "chief's initiation." I'm not at liberty to discuss this because it's only for chiefs to know about, and it would be sacrilege for me to disclose it. I will share *this*, though, because it's public knowledge anyway. It's called "The Chief's Creed."

* * *

During the course of this day, you have been caused to suffer indignities and experience humiliations. This you have accomplished with rare, good grace, and therefore, we now believe it fitting to explain to you why this was done. There was no intent or desire to insult you or demean you. Pointless as it might have seemed to you, there was a valid, time-honored reason behind every single deed, behind each pointed barb.

By experience, by performance, and by testing, you have been this day advanced to E-7. You have one more hurdle to overcome. In the United States Navy—and only in the United States Navy—E-7 carries unique responsibilities. No other armed force throughout the world carries the responsibilities nor grants the privileges to its enlisted personnel comparable to the privileges and responsibilities you are now bound to observe, now expected to fulfill.

Your entire way of life has now been changed. More will be expected of you; more will be demanded of you, not because you're an E-7, but because you are now a chief petty officer.

You have not merely been promoted one pay grade; you have joined an exclusive fraternity. And as in all fraternities, you have a responsibility to your brothers, even as they have a responsibility to you.

Always bear in mind that no other armed force has rate or rank equivalent to that of the United States Navy. Granted that all armed forces have two classes of service, enlisted and commissioned; however, the United States Navy has the distinction of having three—that is, enlisted, bureau-appointed CPO, and commissioned. This is why we in the United States Navy may maintain with pride our feelings of superiority once we have attained the position of E-7.

These privileges, these responsibilities, do not appear in print. They have no official standing; they cannot be referred to by name, number, or file. They exist because for over two hundred years, chiefs before you have freely accepted responsibility beyond the call of printed assignment and have, by their actions and performance, demanded the respect of their seniors, as well as their juniors.

It is now required that you be the fount of wisdom, the ambassador of goodwill, the authority on personnel relations, as well as the technical expert. "Ask the chief" is a household expression in and out of the navy. You are now the *chief.*

The exalted position you have now received—and I use the word *exalted* advisedly—exists because of the attitude, the performance, of chiefs before you. It shall exist only so long as you and your compatriots maintain these standards.

So, this then is why you were caused to experience these things. You were subjected to humiliations to prove to you that humility is good, honorable, a necessary thing that cannot mar you but can, in fact, strengthen you. And in your future as chief petty officer, you will be caused to suffer indignities, to experience humiliations far beyond those imposed upon you today. Bear them with dignity, with the same good graces with which you have borne these this day.

It is our intention to prove these facts to you. It is our intention that you will never forget this day. It is our intention to test you, to try you, to accept you. Your performance has assured us that you will wear your hat with the aplomb and the dignity of your brothers-in-arms. I take a deep, sincere pleasure in clasping your hand and accepting you into our midst. I always endeavored to live up to this. It was an honor to be a chief.

* * *

The next thing that happens is that your life changes. You move out of the enlisted berthing and into the chief's berthing and the CPO mess (or "goat locker," as it's referred to aboard ship).

The racks are wider, mattresses thicker. You have curtains on your rack, and the CPO messcooks make your rack up for you and take care of your laundry. On a Knox-class frigate, there are only about sixteen chiefs. Pretty small fraternity. The chiefs' mess was awesome. We had a couple couches, a small kitchen area, our own head, and a large table with actual chairs. When it was mealtime, we would sit down at the table, and a messcook would take our order and serve it to us on actual plates. No more trays. We'd all sit at the big table and eat together.

Another perk was that we had a refrigerator and cupboards that were well stocked. If it was 2200 and you wanted a sandwich, all you had to do was get up and make one. If you wanted ice cream, it was in the freezer. It was awesome. But it all came at a price. I had more to do as a chief than I ever did as a first class. Much, much more responsibility.

After I became chief, it was clear that I couldn't stay on the *Ouellett*. We already had a chief gunner's mate, and I needed my own ship and a chance to grow as a chief. I called my detailer in Washington, whom I knew well (he'd been one of my C school instructors). The conversation went something like this:

"Mickey, this is Kenny Sams."

"Hey, Kenny, how're you doing these days?"

"Doing pretty good, Mickey, how about you?"

"I'm doing okay. Washington sucks though."

"What can I do for you?"

"Well, Mickey, as you know, I made chief."

"Yeah, I saw that, congratulations."

"Well, I need my own ship and was wondering if there were any billets open out here in Pearl."

"Well, let me take a look . . . Sorry, Kenny, the only sea billet I have open on the West Coast is an amphibious ship out of San Diego. I can send you to her if you want."

"No thanks, Mickey, that'd be a step-down, not what I want to do with my career."

"Okay, Kenny, sit tight. If anything opens up, I'll let you know."

And that was it. No openings on the West Coast other than a *gator freighter*. It would mean I'd have to go back to three-inch guns again, not something I was willing to do.

A couple months passed, and one day the squadron master chief stopped by for a visit, to have lunch with us chiefs. During the meal, somehow my situation came up, and I told him about my conversation with my detailer, Mickey.

The master chief looked at me and said, "That isn't exactly true. I happen to know there's a frigate here in Pearl that desperately needs a chief gunner's mate."

My jaw just about dropped.

He said, "She's the USS *Rathburne*, and she's over in the shipyards. Why don't you take a walk over there and check her out. If there are any problems, or you need help with Mickey, just give me a call."

I couldn't believe it. There was actually a frigate in Pearl that needed a chief gunner's mate. That same afternoon, I took a long walk to where she was. I introduced myself to the officer of the deck, and he immediately called the chief's quarters, and within about a minute, one of the chiefs came up to the quarterdeck and took me down to the CPO mess. I met most of the chiefs, and they told me about the ship and what to expect if I got orders to her. Then they let me walk around the ship on my own. The first place I went, of course, was to the gun mount.

There was no gun mount there. As it turned out, the *Rathburne*'s old mount was in such bad shape they decided to replace it. She was going to get a brand-new one. A gunner's mate's dream come true. One other thing I noticed was, there weren't any gunner's mates around (more about that later). I returned to the chiefs' mess, thanked everyone, and left.

Early the next morning, I was on the phone with my detailer.

"Hello, Mickey, this is Kenny Sams again."

"Hey, Kenny, what's happening? I still haven't found you a ship yet, buddy."

"That's okay, Mickey, I found one myself."

"What?" I asked him to check on the USS *Rathburne*, and sure enough, he found her; he just missed it before.

"Are you sure it's what you want?" he asked.

"Absolutely," I replied.

"Okay, buddy, you're penciled in. You should see your orders in about two weeks."

He was a man of his word, and sure enough, about two weeks later, my orders showed up.

A "same port" transfer is a whole lot easier than to a different home port. First of all, it's more of an administrative thing than a physical thing. I didn't have to have my household goods shipped, and we were able to stay in our quarters in base housing. All I had to do was move my gear off one ship and take it onto another. Secondly, it's almost "instantaneous"; it can be done very quickly.

The *Rathburne*, FF-1057, was another Knox-class frigate, just like the *Meyerkord* and the *Ouellett*. They were all pretty much identical, so I didn't have to learn my way around. There were minor differences, but not much. The gun was in the same place, all the compartments were pretty much the same, and the entire layout of the ship was the same. I blended in pretty quickly with the other chiefs and was an accepted member of the mess.

The ship still had about three months left in the yards, then it would be a "shakedown cruise," then more time in the yards to correct anything that didn't work as it should.

I didn't do much for about two weeks. I had to get a feel for my gun crew and everything I was responsible for. I mostly went through the overhaul maintenance schedule and assessed where it said we were and where we actually were, overhaul-wise. I didn't want to come out of overhaul with a lot of problems that should have been corrected but weren't.

In the meantime, the reason I didn't see any gunner's mates on my visit to the *Rathburne* before I took the orders was that the gunner's mate first class let them go on "early liberty." According to him, he was in charge of the overhaul maintenance schedule, and the gunner's mates were "ahead" of overhaul. He had the chain of command convinced that they were way ahead of schedule.

I looked around our spaces and was convinced otherwise. The magazines hadn't been painted (you can't paint in an ammunition magazine if you have live ammo present; it needs to be done when it's empty). We had other spaces—passageways, the armory, pyrotechnic lockers, and the berthing compartment— that hadn't been touched. I didn't want to come across as a "total asshole chief," but I had to do something before our time ran out and we'd end up "fucked" when the ship came out of the yards. I decided to go ahead and be the "asshole." It was pretty much the only choice I had. Like the squadron master chief said, "They desperately needed a chief gunner's mate."

After about two weeks on board, I kept the gunner's mates behind after morning quarters were over. I laid it out to them that the "early liberty" was over and that we had a lot of work to do and that they could plan on "extended" working hours. As I figured, I was pretty "unpopular" with my gun crew. I could see that it was going to be an "uphill" battle, especially without the support of my first class, not to mention the fact that some of the chiefs liked him and didn't care for me being so heavy-handed with my crew.

It was a grueling three months. I had to stay on top of everything. I wasn't home very much.

When we finally finished overhaul, we had a brand-new gun that worked perfectly, all our spaces were immaculate, everything was like new, and we started our sea trials. We loaded out our ammo at the ammo piers and were on our way. The gun performed perfectly, and the workload on my crew was pretty light. All they had to do was keep up the maintenance on the gun and keep our spaces clean. Lo and behold, when we returned to port, and the other divisions were dealing with problems that hadn't been corrected during overhaul, the gunner's mates were going on "early liberty." Things were a lot better between me and my crew after that.

A few months after we left the shipyards, my first class got a transfer, and we got a new one, Jack. He was a godsend to me. He had a very even demeanor, knew his shit about the gun, and was very squared away. He turned out to be a wonderful example for the rest of the gun gang.

Life in the gunnery world was going great. Unfortunately, for me, it was to be short-lived. Within about six months after reporting aboard, Jack was selected for chief. He actually stayed on board. Rather than transferring, he took over as the ASROC (antisubmarine rocket launcher) chief, and I stayed with the gun mount. We got to be very good friends, and as it turned out, he and his family lived about a block away from me in base housing. He had a daughter about the same age as my youngest, and they became friends also.

A few months later, a new gunner's mate first class reported aboard. His name was Scott. Again, I got lucky. He was squared away, knew his shit about the gun mount, made an excellent mount captain, had an even temperament, and got along great with the gun crew. He accepted my leadership with good grace and kept me well informed. I still hold him in high regard.

A few months later, we were being deployed to the Middle East. I was tasked with developing a ship's self-defense plan, which required a lot of research and attending seminars on terrorism. It took a long time to write it, but in the end, the captain accepted it, and it became the ship's policy. Then the training phase began. By the time we reached the Persian Gulf, I had trained a proficient ship's self-defense force, and we were ready.

This deployment was a lot different than any I'd been on. There were very few liberty ports, and our mission was to assist and escort merchant ships that flew the American flag and traversed the Gulf.

At this point, there were hostilities between Iraq and Iran, and both countries were trying to disrupt each other's shipping. Both countries had military planes that they used to attack ships. Once again, we were in a designated combat zone and back on condition 3 gun mount watches.

Rarely did a day go by that we weren't called to general quarters and would have to load the gun system up to the transfer trays because we had inbound possibly hostile aircraft.

Loading a five-inch gun mount to the transfer trays is relatively easy. The mount captain pushes a button, and everything happens automatically. The *hard* part is unloading it. There was no reverse to the loading system. All the projectiles and powder cans had to be manually removed from the system. The entire loading system could hold twelve rounds, excluding the loader drums in the projectile magazine below the carrier room. High explosive projectiles weighed about seventy-eight pounds each, and the powder cans weighed about forty-six pounds each. That's twelve powders and twelve projectiles that had to be removed from the gun system and physically carried back down to the magazine. All on a ship that was pitching and rolling.

It would take us about half an hour to get all the ammo back to the magazine and properly stowed. I can tell you, it got pretty monotonous day after day, week after week.

There are no liberty ports in the Persian Gulf. We would steam for months at a time without pulling into a liberty port. The only friendly port was Bahrain. The navy didn't want ships in port because we were susceptible to small boat attacks. We actually pulled into Bahrain twice.

The first time was after being at sea for over three months. We pulled into the harbor, anchored out, and had .50-caliber machine guns manned the whole time. We only stayed one night, then it was back out into the Gulf. The one thing the ship did while we were there was that they had a floating barge brought alongside and tied up to us. We rigged the accommodation ladder, and the captain allowed us to take cases of beer and ice chests down to it, put the chiefs in charge of it, and allowed every crew member to have two beers each. I can tell you, there was quite a lot of profiteering among the crew that night. Crew members who didn't drink were selling their beers to crew members who did.

As a chief, I wouldn't divulge where I got my information, but I was told that the going rate was $20 a beer. God bless them—if it had been up to me, they'd each gotten at least a six-pack; they deserved it. Actually, I was one of the chiefs who was keeping the tally, and I might have forgotten to write some of it down. Damn my forgetfulness.

The second time we pulled into Bahrain was about a month or so after that. This time we moored pierside close to the USS *Lasalle*. She was a repair ship that was permanently assigned to the Persian Gulf. She had dentists and doctors on board, and some of the crew needed to see them. They also had repair capabilities for our ship, and there were a few things that needed attention. I think we spent two days there. There was not a lot to do in Bahrain except to go to the marketplace (where the primary souvenirs were gold jewelry and perfume) or go to the American Service Unit to have a few beers at the servicemen's clubs. It was a short stay in port, then back out into the Gulf.

The perfume that everyone bought in Bahrain wasn't actually perfume; it was the essence that went into "making" perfume. It was in tiny little glass bottles and was supposed to be diluted with alcohol before use. It was relatively cheap, and you could buy any perfume that was on the market in the world. I think every crewman bought some for their wives or girlfriends.

After we left the Gulf, still with about a month to go before returning to Pearl, one of the guys in the forward crew's compartment dropped a bottle of it, and it shattered. The forward crew's quarters smelled like a whorehouse for the rest of the deployment. Actually, it wasn't exactly "unpleasant." I would say it was an improvement over the usual smell of "sweaty sailor." Chanel No. 5 is so much better.

I did make it into Bahrain one other time, but it wasn't with the ship. We had been out on patrol and were heading to Bahrain but weren't pulling in. We were just getting close so the *Desert Duck*, an SH-3 Sea King helicopter that was stationed in

Bahrain, could bring our mail out to us. Our flight deck wasn't large enough for them to land, so they'd hover above it and send our mail down on a "wire."

I had been up forward all day working in the carrier room (it was past knock-off), so I went aft to the chief's quarters to wait for supper. I sat down on one of the couches and almost immediately started getting pains in my left chest, which would shoot down my left arm. One of the other chiefs noticed me grimacing, asked me what the matter was, and when I told him, he called up to the bridge and had the word passed for the chief corpsman to lay to the chief's quarters.

"Doc" came in and started checking me over, thinking maybe I was having a heart attack. When the executive officer showed up and asked the doc what was going on, Doc told him he wasn't quite sure yet.

Then the XO said, "Get him up to the flight deck and on the helo."

I was still having chest pains as they helped me up to the flight deck. Senior Chief Packer was one of them, and as we were walking, he shoved a fifty-dollar bill in my pocket. Aboard ship we never carried money around; there was no need for it. Later, I was sure glad he did that.

We got up to the flight deck. The helo was hovering about two hundred feet above us and sending down "the wire." It was a sling attached to a cable that was attached to a winch above the side door of the helo. I remember thinking to myself at that moment, "You can't possibly be serious."

The flight deck crew helped me get the sling on around my chest and under my armpits, and away I went. The helo banked away from the ship with me dangling about two hundred feet below. I looked down, and the only thing below me was the ocean, with the ship fading into the distance. It took about a minute for them to hoist me up, and I was never so glad to have something solid under my feet as I did right then.

The helo crew had me lie on a bench right across from the open door as we flew to Bahrain. The trip took about thirty minutes, and we finally landed at the Bahrain airport. They had an ambulance waiting for me and rushed me to the hospital.

Once in the emergency room, they checked my heart but couldn't find any signs of cardiac arrest. Then they did a bunch of other tests. By this time the pain was gone, and I was feeling better. They held me there for hours but couldn't find anything wrong. I asked the doctor what he thought was going on, and he told me that it was probably "gas." He said that sometimes you could get gas built up so much that it feels like a heart attack. I guess I had "gas," and shit, look where it got me. Miles and miles away from my ship, in a foreign hospital, with no change of clothing, and how long would it be before I could get back to my ship?

They released me from the hospital and got me to the American Service Unit, which was kind of a small navy base. I checked in, they assigned me quarters, and then I just had to wait until the ship came within helicopter range again.

I hadn't eaten anything since lunch, and since I was feeling better and hungry, I went to the club and ordered a steak dinner. It was awesome. Steaks on the ship are okay, but it had been months since I'd had one that good. I remember thinking about the guys on the ship and what they'd had for dinner. Yeah, I was gloating to myself. Oh yeah, I had a couple of beers too.

The next morning, I went over to admin to find out what my status was. They told me the *Rathburne* was too far away to transport me back, so I just had to be patient. They'd let me know. I ended up being there for three days when they told me my ship was on its way and would be within range in about six hours. I took a shuttle back to the airfield and the *Desert Duck* hangar, sat, and waited.

Eventually, one of the flight crew came and got me and said, "Okay, Chief, we're ready to roll."

I got on board, and we were off again. It was about a forty-five-minute flight, but there she was, the *Rathburne*. She looked so tiny from up there.

The helo hovered again, about two hundred feet above the flight deck. The aircrewman put the harness back on me and shoved me out the door. Down I went onto the flight deck. Those guys were good. They landed me gently on the flight deck, exactly in the middle, and I was home. It felt so good to be back. I'll tell you what—I found it less stressful to enter and exit a helicopter when it was on the ground rather than two hundred feet in the air.

Our time in the Gulf eventually came to an end. It was a relief to go through the Straits of Hormuz one last time. We were headed for Australia. We sailed south to the southern coast and then east to Melbourne.

Some of the crew had arranged to fly their wives down, since we'd be spending a week in Melbourne then a week in Sydney. I happened to be one of them, along with about three of the other chiefs and a few of the officers.

We pulled into Melbourne, which was no easy feat. The wind kept pushing us away from the pier, and all they had was little pusher boats to help us. I didn't see any real tugboats. After about three attempts and heavy strains on our working lines, we were moored. And there on the pier was my wife along with about a dozen other wives.

Australia was going to be one of our last port calls for the deployment. We were supposed to out-chop for Pearl from there, with a stop in Fiji. I chose to take leave in Melbourne and fly back to Pearl with my wife.

She and I spent a week in Melbourne, which was a fantastic town. The people were so nice, and it was so relaxing to be ashore again and to be with my wife after five months away. We took a train up to Sydney to spend a week there before flying back to Hawaii.

(A side story here. When we boarded the train from Melbourne to Sydney, we took our seats, which were old-fashioned, two-person seats that faced each other. As we got on the train, I noticed a sign on the bathroom door that said, "Do not use the restroom while train is at the station." I didn't think too much of it at the time. We took our seats, and after a while, the train left the station and headed for Sydney. An hour or so later, I had to use the restroom, so I got up, went to the restroom door, lifted the lid on the toilet, then I understood the sign. I was looking down at railroad ties zipping by. I wouldn't want to be a railroad worker there, let alone walk down the railroad tracks.)

We finally got to Sydney and got a hotel room. It was wonderful to sleep in a large bed and eat in restaurants after so many months at sea. We spent a week in Sydney, toured all around, and visited the Opera House and downtown. It was exciting. Eventually, we had to leave it and catch a flight back to Hawaii. I was able to book a seat on the same flight my wife was on; I was actually able to get the seat next to her. Our plane was a 747. It was great; they even had a bar on board. This was my first experience flying on a commercial transpacific flight. All the other flights I'd made were on military transports. It was a luxury to me.

We landed in Hawaii. Our friends picked us up at the airport and took us home. It was wonderful seeing my daughters again. It's amazing how much a child can grow in just six months. About two weeks later, the *Rathburne* returned to Pearl. This was the first time I ever had a ship "catch up" to me. It'd always been the other way around.

It wasn't too long after this that Hurricane Ewa hit. We had been out on local ops and had just returned to Pearl Harbor. We had tied up, they passed liberty call, and everyone who didn't have duty headed ashore. My guys wanted to go to the EM club for a beer and invited me, their chief, to come along. Of course, I obliged. We were sitting in the club enjoying our beer when all of a sudden, a sailor came into the club and yelled, "Hey, everyone, all the ships are flying the recall pennant!"

We all went outside to look, and sure enough, all the ships were flying "recall." What this means is that all crew members need to return to the ship because there's some kind of emergency. This left me with a moral decision to make. Should I pretend I didn't see it and go home to my wife and children, or should I return to the ship? Of course, I chose to go back to the ship.

I walked onto the quarterdeck and asked the officer of the deck what was going on. He told me that we had a hurricane bearing down on Hawaii and all the ships had to evacuate.

I thanked him, went out onto the pier to the phone booth, called my wife, and told her what was going on. She was scared, I was scared, but I had no choice in what I had to do. I told her I loved her and to take good care of the kids. She was a pretty intelligent woman and had a good head on her shoulders, so I wasn't too worried. I went back on board and started preparations to get underway.

During a hurricane, it's standard nautical practice for ships to get underway to ride out the storm out to sea. They stand a better chance of surviving there rather than tied up to a pier. If a storm surge is strong enough, it can literally pick a ship up and set it onto a pier or tip it over.

When it was our turn, we cast off and headed out to sea in line with the rest of the squadrons. We stowed our lines on the way out, and when we cleared the harbor entrance, all hell broke loose. Almost immediately, we were taking water over the bow. I went below to the carrier room, the compartment just below the gun mount, to make sure everything was lashed down. When I opened the hatch, the first thing I saw was water pouring down from the gun mount. Then it hit me. In our haste to get underway, we had forgotten to pump up the gun-port seal. If we left it like it was, the carrier room would be flooded in no time.

I grabbed a pump, secured the hatch, and headed up to the bridge. Then I went up to the officer of the deck and explained the situation. He asked me what course of action we could take, so I explained to him that if he could alter the ship's course for just a couple minutes so the waves would come in from the stern, I could pump up the seal. He thought for a minute, got on the growler to the captain (who was below in his stateroom), hung up the handset, ordered a course change, then said to me, "Okay, Chief, you have three minutes, so be quick."

As the ship came about, I ran down to the foc'sle to the front of the gun mount, attached the pump as quickly as I could, then pumped my ass off. Even though the ship had altered course, there were still waves coming over the bow, just not as strong as before.

Just as I was finishing up, the OOD yelled down on a bullhorn, "Chief! Time's up. I have to change course. Now!"

I grabbed the pump and ran as fast as I could back to the hatch, but I wasn't fast enough. A huge wave came over the bow, picked me up, and slammed me into the closed hatch. As the ship rose on the next swell, and the water ran off the deck, I was able to get the hatch open and get through it just as another wave crashed over the bow. I got the hatch closed and dogged down, and there I stood, out of breath and soaked. I went back up to the bridge to let the OOD know that I had been successful. He took one look at me and apologized for having to change course, then he thanked me for what I had done. I went back down below to the chief's quarters to change into dry clothes.

As I entered the mess, everyone looked at me and said, "What the fuck happened to you?"

"I was just out playing in the water!" I said.

We were out there for about three days. It was a pretty rough ride, but when we pulled back in, the skies were clear and the water calm. My wife picked me up, and while we were driving home, we discussed our experiences during the storm. As it turned out, the area we lived in was without electrical power. We didn't get it back for several days.

One thing about the whole episode that pisses me off to this day is that they were expecting a strong storm surge on our side of the island. The navy housing we lived in was right at the entrance to Pearl Harbor. Our house was maybe five hundred yards from the ocean and maybe fifteen feet above sea level. The navy ordered an evacuation of our housing area, and base security was going door-to-door telling everyone to evacuate. My wife later told me that she and our kids hid from security when they knocked on our door because she didn't want to evacuate. I was furious with her. I thought she was smarter than that.

Hurricane Ewa happened just before Thanksgiving. It made for interesting and memorable holiday celebrations. We had no power, so we cooked our turkey on the barbecue and cooked everything else on a camp stove. I took ice chests to the ship to get ice from the ship's ice machine to keep our food cold, and a friend of mine who lived on the other side of Pearl Harbor, and still had electricity, baked us an apple pie and a pumpkin pie. All in all, we had a wonderful and memorable Thanksgiving.

I spent about another year on the *Rathburne* doing local ops and had one trip to the West Coast for a RIMPAC (Rim of the Pacific exercises). As it turned out, she was to be my last ship. My seashore rotation was up, and it was time to go back to shore.

When that time came, I was back on the phone with my detailer, trying to find a shore duty billet in Pearl Harbor. To my dismay, there weren't any. My detailer told me he wanted me in Washington, DC, to be a detailer with him. He tried to convince me that it'd be a smart career move and that he "really" needed me there. Washington, DC, was the *last* place I wanted to go. Once again, I had to find my own billet.

I finally found one at Fleet Training Group on Ford Island. It was "neutral" duty—which meant it didn't count as sea duty and didn't count as shore duty—and after my tour there, I'd have to go to a shore duty billet, and it would be years before I could go to another ship. What a catch-22. I ended up taking the orders to FTG. Anything to keep from going to DC.

# Chapter Four

# Destroyer Life

Destroyer sailors, my shipmates, were the finest men I've ever known—not just because they were my shipmates, but because they were "all" good men. Life on a destroyer is tough, and they were a *tough* bunch of guys. We were all a big family and helped each other in every way possible, whether it was work-related or personal. They were "all" my brothers. If you needed something, all you had to do was ask.

A destroyer is "small." It's only 438 feet long and 46 feet wide at its widest. There are about 225 guys on board. You're cooped up together, for sometimes months at a time. You share a lot of experiences, like storms, liberty ports, and just day-to-day life. Everybody knew everybody. It didn't matter what rate you were; we all shared meals together and would congregate on the fantail together after the ship's work was done and after the evening meal. I can still remember many of their names, all four crews. I even keep in touch with some of them. Being a member of a ship's crew is a "lifetime" thing. It doesn't end when you leave a ship.

Destroyermen work hard. When you're in a combat zone, there isn't much "leisure" time. If you're not standing a watch or maintaining the ship, you're "off" time is spent sleeping. When you're not in a combat zone, there are fewer watches to be stood, so you have a little more free time.

Sailors are *masters* at passing time. They read a lot. If there's a popular book out, and one of the crew has it, you can bet it's going to change hands more than any book in any library. There's also the "bodybuilders," the guys who work out every day. For some reason, that never appealed to me. Then there were the games. I remember a Monopoly game that went on in gun plot that lasted two weeks (played only in the evening). Poker games? Gambling is against the Uniform Code of Military Justice, so it's illegal in the navy. That didn't stop the sailors though. There were poker games all over the ship every night, not just on one of my ships but *all* of them. The officers just turned a blind eye and let it alone. Hell, I'm sure they had their own poker games.

The biggest one I ever saw was in the chiefs' mess on one of my ships. It happened *every* night and would go on until the wee hours of the morning (chiefs don't stand underway watches, unless they choose to). I've seen lots of sailors practice musical instruments, guitars, banjos, saxophones, trumpets, you name it. I was a guitar player myself and spent countless hours in my off-time practicing. I still play to this day. Some sailors built models. I was stationed with a senior chief that built a four-foot-long model ship during one deployment. The details were fantastic. Anything to pass the time.

Often, especially in the evenings, a lot of us would gather on the fantail, which seemed to be our social gathering place. We'd just stand around and shoot the shit and smoke cigarettes. A lot of the time, there'd be seagulls or albatrosses following the ship, waiting for us to throw trash over the side. The seagulls would land on the trash bags and tear into them. Sometimes sharks would do the same. It was interesting to watch. My favorite was when a school of porpoises would join us and play in our wake or our bow wave. I loved watching them. So did everyone else. There was also other "wildlife" out there. We would often see whales and orcas. One time I saw a giant manta ray probably twenty feet across swimming between our ship and an oiler that we were refueling with that was probably fifty feet away. It was beautiful to see.

After the sun went down, you could see the water in our wake come alive with bioluminescence. The plankton in the water would give off a greenish glow. It was beautiful and mesmerizing. Sunsets were usually pretty spectacular. A lot of the crew would show up on the fantail just to watch the sunset. I've never seen a sunset on land that can compare to the ones I've seen at sea.

## Berthing

The berthing compartments on destroyers are a bit cramped. The racks are in tier 3 high. The preferred rack is the middle, then second choice is the bottom, and last choice is the top. Racks are assigned based on seniority, not necessarily by rank, but by "time on board." The only exception is a petty officer first class. Lockers are your racks—or should I say, racks are your lockers. They're seven feet long, three feet wide, and about eight inches deep. The entire top lifts up with hinges on the back and has a support bar to hold it open. When closed, your mattress is on top, and that's your rack.

Berthing compartments vary in size and are segregated into divisions. On the *Reeves*, the Second Division compartment consisted of sixteen racks. On the three frigates I was on, the entire weapons department was berthed in the forward crews' quarters and berthed about sixty sailors, gunners, fire controlmen, and boatswain's mates. There was a smaller compartment forward of that, which berthed about sixteen; it was home to the sonarmen, torpedomen, and ASROC gunner's mates. There were various other berthing compartments for the snipes, operations guys, supply, and navigation. They were pretty much throughout the ship.

Shipboard berthing compartments are "home" to a sailor, but they can get pretty uncomfortable at times, particularly if the ship is on "water hours" and the guys can't take showers. It can get a little (*a lot*) ripe. Also, there are lot of sailors that *snore*. Imagine trying to sleep in a room with fifty-nine other guys with about half of them snoring. Earplugs worked wonders.

* * *

I have to pause here to tell you my favorite "berthing" story. I was on my first ship, the *Reeves*. I had a middle rack, and my third class, Dave, had the rack below me. We were in Vietnam at the time, underway. I was a boot seaman and still learning. One night we got into some heavy seas, and there was something rolling around in my locker, which was also my rack. We were trying to sleep, but it was pretty rough.

Dave said to me, "Goddamn, what the fuck do you have rolling around in your locker?"

I said, "Oh, it's probably just the grenades."

"Man . . ." He came unglued. He jumped out of his rack, turned the berthing compartment lights on, and had me get up and open my locker.

There, rolling around in my locker, were three concussion grenades. Concussion grenades are carried by ships for defense against swimmers that could attack a ship. They're about two and a half inches thick and about six inches tall. They're made of TNT (trinitrotoluene). When stored, the body of the grenade is stored separately from the fuses (or detonators). Before use, you have to screw the detonator into the TNT body, then they're ready to go. All you have to do is pull the pin and drop them over the side, then *boom*, they explode.

About three days prior, the officer of the deck, on the bridge, had me bring him up three grenades. We were supposed to have a general quarters drill that day, and they wanted them for "simulated" torpedo hits. If you drop them over the side, about six feet away from the ship, when they explode, the whole ship shudders and you can hear it throughout the ship. The navy used them all the time. It brought a sense of "realism" to the drill. Well, the drill got canceled, and as I was standing in the mess line to get my supper, they passed the word for me to "lay to the bridge."

When I got up there, the OOD handed the grenades back to me to restow in the magazine. I didn't have the keys to the magazine (one of the other gunner's mates had them), so I took them down to my locker, so they'd be locked up and went back to the mess line. Well, I forgot about them. When Dave saw them, not only did I have to immediately take them back to the magazine, but Dave—being the kindhearted mentor that he was and always looking out for me—gave me four more hours of extra duty in the fire room. They were getting to know me pretty well down there.

When a ship's underway and taps sound, the berthing compartment lights are shut off and red lights are turned on.

There are two reasons for this. The first is that throughout the night, sailors have to get up and stand their watches. If you have the *midwatch*, you have to relieve the 2000–2400 watch at 2345 hours. If you have the *rev watch*, you have to relieve the midwatch at 0345 hours. You need light to see to get dressed.

The second reason is so you can see when you go topside. It's dark, and if you were in white light, you wouldn't be able to see shit for about ten minutes. In red light, your retinas dilate. So, when you go out into the dark, you can see immediately. Underway, the berthing compartment can be pretty comforting, aside from all the snoring. You're in your own little space, the ships rolling and pitching, and there's the hum of the ventilation system and the engines. The ship vibrates, and you can hear the sound of the waves crashing into the side of the ship. To a sailor, it's like a lullaby, and it puts you to sleep pretty quickly. The only exception is if you're in heavy seas, but even then, it's pretty easy to sleep once you know how.

In port it's a different story. The engines are shut down, the rolling and pitching aren't there, and then you have the liberty party returning to the ship at all hours of the night. Drunk sailors are seldom quiet.

My story about that goes like this (and this is a hundred-percent true story):

While I was on the *Reeves*, we had a gunner's mate named Joe in the division. Joe wasn't a very squared-away sailor; in fact, he wasn't the sharpest knife in the drawer. We were in port, had been on liberty, returned to the ship, and turned in. Joe came back from liberty way after the rest of us and was literally three-sheets-to-the-wind drunk. Maybe more. He stumbled down the ladder into the berthing compartment, pretty much waking everyone up. He stumbled around the compartment for a little bit, then all of a sudden, it got really quiet.

Then we heard it, the sound of water hitting the floor. Dave, my third class, turned on his bunk light, and there was Joe, pissing in the middle of the compartment, right next to Dave's rack.

Dave was out of his rack like a gunshot, yelling at Joe, "You motherfucker, get that shit cleaned up, right now!"

Joe knelt down and, with his hand, pushed the puddle under Dave's rack. The next thing I saw was Dave punching Joe hard in the face. Joe fell back against a locker.

Dave told him again, "Get that shit cleaned up!"

Well, Joe did as he was told and grabbed the nearest thing to a towel he could find, which happened to be Dave's shirt hanging next to his rack and proceeded to wipe up the piss.

*Wham!* Dave hit him again and threw Joe into his own rack. I got up and helped Dave clean up the mess, but the compartment smelled like piss the rest of the week. Joe was in the shits with the rest of us for quite a while after that, especially Dave.

## Messdecks

Enough about berthing compartments. Let's talk about meals and messdecks aboard destroyers. The messdecks are where the crew comes together three times a day for meals and again at about 1900 hours for "movie call." There are eighteen to twenty tables, which are secured to the deck on stanchions, and attached to each table are six swivel seats. There's a lip around the table about an eighth of an inch high, supposedly to keep your tray from sliding off the table (doesn't always work).

When you go through the mess line, first you pick up a tray from the stack, then your silverware, which you put in your pocket, then proceed through the serving line. The cooks are behind the line dishing out the food, then you carry your tray to the "cow," or "tits" (milk machine), and get your drink. Then you find an open seat, sit down, and eat.

There are several variations to this routine. In heavy seas, when you sit down to eat, you hold on to your tray with one hand and eat with the other, all the while either wrapping your legs around the table stanchion or spreading them wide apart to keep you in your seat. If you need to get up to refill your drink, you take your tray with you.

I learned something on my first ship. If you take a paper napkin, wet it, and spread it out on the table, then set your tray on it, it'd stay put, up to a point. You could always tell who the new guys were. They'd set their tray down on a table then go to the cow to get a glass of milk. About thirty seconds later, *crash*—their tray was on the deck. Everyone would clap and cheer; the new guy would be chasing his "beanie weenies" across the messdecks. The new guy would have to clean it up, go back to the end of the mess line, and try it again. Sometimes, when it was really rough, the cooks couldn't cook. They wouldn't be able to keep anything on the grill or anything in the pots.

During those times, we usually had "horse cock" (bologna) and cheese sandwiches, with potato chips, or tuna sandwiches.

Just like in a family, mealtimes were a time for the crew to come together and socialize. That's one of the ways we all got to know each other.

The food on a ship ranges in quality. There are good "feeders" and not-so-good feeders. I was fortunate to serve on two *excellent* feeders, one okay feeder, and one crap feeder. I'm not going to name names, but the *Reeves* and the *Rathburne* were excellent feeders. The food was, for the most part, wonderful. The food on the *Ouellett* was okay, so we'll leave it at that.

Breakfast was usually bacon or sausage, sometimes fried horse cock and eggs, oatmeal, cereal, pancakes, fruit, cinnamon rolls or doughnuts, hash browns, and milk or coffee.

Lunch and supper varied. One day it might be spaghetti; the next, grilled cheese sandwiches; the next, fried chicken; the next, roast beef; the next, rabbit. Lunch and supper always included a vegetable, starch (like potatoes or macaroni), and dessert, which could be anything from cake to apple pie. Occasionally, we'd get steak and lobster.

The food they served was sometimes regulated by what supplies were available.

* * *

A story here. When I was on the *Reeves*, my second deployment, we went on a "show the flag" cruise. We left the Philippines with the USS *Schofield* (I believe) and an oiler. (I think the oiler was the *Hassayampa* or could have been the *Misspillion*, I'm not sure.) We loaded up as many supplies as we could and headed out for the Indian Ocean. We were gone for about three months, without rendezvousing with any other supply ships or docking at any US Navy bases for resupply. Our trip took us up the eastern coast of Africa and along the southern coast of the Middle East.

I can't remember the order that we ran out of food, but I think it went like this. First, we ran out of fresh milk, so we started drinking powdered milk. Then it was bread, so the cooks started baking bread. The next to go were fresh vegetables, so we started eating canned vegetables. The next thing was eggs, so we switched to *powdered* eggs. Then the fresh meat started running out, so we had to eat *canned* meat. Then all of the above started running out, even flour, so they couldn't bake bread or pastries anymore. When we pulled into Mombasa, Kenya, the supply officer went ashore and tried to get supplies. We ended up with this dark bread—tiny loaves that tasted like shit and were as hard as a rock. He was able to get some vegetables, but they ended up being infested with maggots.

We were leaving Mombasa, Kenya. It was lunchtime, and the cooks put out a pan of sliced cucumbers, onions, and vinegar. I was on my second helping when I noticed one of the cucumber seeds *moving*. Upon closer inspection, I realized it wasn't a seed at all—it was a maggot! I took my tray up to one of the cooks. He looked at it and immediately pulled them off the serving line. I believe they had to throw out most of the fresh vegetables we'd received. Our boxed cereal, cornflakes, Rice Krispies, etc. were infested with weevils that you had to pick out after you poured the powdered milk on.

All in all, the cooks did the best they could, God bless 'em. I remember, probably the last three weeks of the cruise, just about all the canned meat had been used up, except for SPAM. We got SPAM for breakfast, SPAM for lunch, SPAM for supper. It took me years before I could eat SPAM again.

The messdecks were also where they showed the ship's movie every night. After the messdecks were cleaned up, the crew would start drifting in to get a good seat. The best place was right in front of the screen, but you had to get there early to get those seats. The navy always got "first run" movies, so whatever was showing at movie theatres, was also sent to our troops. Movies were swapped from ship to ship, so you didn't see the same movie over and over. The only exception was when you were forward deployed and didn't have any other ships around to swap with. I remember a few times like this. After seeing the same movie three or four times, the messdecks would be pretty much empty for movie call.

We always had "popcorn." Every ship I served on had a popcorn machine, and the ship's servicemen would start popping it about thirty minutes before movie call. You just can't watch a movie without popcorn. It's the law.

## Laundry

Laundry on a destroyer can be a "hit or miss" thing. The ship doesn't always have the fresh water to spare to do it. Sometimes we'd go weeks without clean laundry. In a berthing compartment is a laundry locker; inside are several large laundry bags. You put your dirty laundry in the locker, and once a week, the designated compartment cleaner would bag up the dirty clothes and take them down to the ship's laundry. It was always a good thing to have your name stenciled on your clothing; otherwise, you probably wouldn't ever see them again.

In the ship's laundry, they'd empty a laundry bag into an industrial-size washing machine, throw in some harsh laundry detergent, run the clothes through a wash cycle and a rinse cycle, and throw them in a large industrial dryer. Then just before the clothes were dry, they'd take them out, stuff them back in the laundry bag, then throw them on a pile for a couple of days. You can only imagine what they smelled like when we got them back—*very sour*. Thank God we had an ironing board and iron in the berthing compartment. Also, the ship's laundry wouldn't do civilian clothes—that was up to us.

When I made chief, it was a different story. The chiefs' messcooks would take the dirty laundry to the ship's laundry, and when it was done, they'd bring it back, nicely pressed and on hangers, and they'd hang them on our lockers for us. Yeah, being a chief had its perks, but remember, I paid my dues to get there.

## Routine

The general routine on a destroyer goes like this:

Reveille goes at 0600 hours. The ship's master-at-arms goes through the ship and turns on all the white lights in the berthing compartments. You don't necessarily have to get right out of your rack, but if you want breakfast—and believe me, you do—you better roll out. Breakfast goes from 0630 to 0745.

Next, at 0800 hours is "quarters"—that's where you assemble in ranks to get the plan of the day, roll call, and inspected. Officers call goes at 0745—that's where the division officers and department heads muster with the executive officer to get any last-minute instructions to pass on to their divisions.

After the division officer addresses his division, all hands are dismissed until 0830. Then they pass: "Turn to commence ship's work." That's when we go to work, whatever it may be, mostly doing maintenance on the ship's gun and our assigned spaces. At 1115 hours, they pass the word: "Mess gear, clear the messdecks, early lunch for cooks, messcooks, and the oncoming watch." Then at 1130 hours, it's, "Knock off ship's work, lunch for the crew."

*Yay, lunchtime.*

We hurry down, grab lunch, then find a quiet place (for gunner's mates, it was the carrier room), turn the lights off, and take a quick nap. At 1230 hours, it's now "Turn-to, continue ship's work." We wake up and go back to work. Knockoff goes at 1630 hours. That's free time—you can do whatever you want for the rest of the day. At 1700, it is early supper for cooks, messcooks, and the oncoming watch. Supper for the crew is at 1730 until 1830 hours, then movie call is at 1900 hours, then taps at 2200 hours.

Mealtimes never change, unless they're delayed because of general quarters. Sundays are "holiday routine." The entire day is yours unless you have a watch to stand. Sunday mealtimes are the same as during the week. When a ship is in port, the crew has both Saturday and Sunday off, unless you have duty, which is usually every third day for a three-section duty or every fourth day in the case of a four-section duty.

Underway, you work Monday through Saturday, six days a week. The ship's routine can vary from the norm, and it "does" quite a bit. There's always refueling with oilers, flight quarters to launch or recover the helo, replenishment with supply ships, general quarters for drills, general quarters for gunnery exercises—always something going on. I'm pretty sure this routine is the same on "all" ships—at least it was the same on all of mine.

## Watches

Watches, watches, and watches. Sailors stand a lot of watches. On a peacetime steaming destroyer, *somebody* had to drive the ship and keep the engines running. It's not all leisure time on a destroyer. The bridge watch consisted of an officer of the deck, which was usually the department heads. Then there's the junior officer of the deck, usually one of the division officers. Then there's the boatswain's mate of the watch, usually a petty officer second or third class, who coordinated the enlisted watch section and made sure the rotation between watch stations happens. Then the other enlisted watch stations: helmsman, lee helmsman, messenger of the watch, forward lookout, port lookout, starboard lookout, and after lookout. There was also a quartermaster and a signalman. That was twelve people just to man the bridge.

There was also the Combat Information Center. I'm not sure exactly how many guys were in there. I only went into CIC when I had to; it was frowned upon to go there. I do know there was a CIC officer, probably four operations specialists, and a couple of sonarmen. Radio central was also manned 24-7. I believe it was two radiomen per watch. After steering was also manned by just one person constantly when underway.

Damage Control Central was also manned constantly, along with a roving watch that checked tank levels and machinery spaces. The engine room and fire room were also manned. (I can't tell you how many guys it was. I was a gunner's mate, and since I had to do extra duty down there when I was a seaman, I always avoided going down there. I wasn't cut out to be a snipe. It was hot and loud down there.) Underway, though, the watch section was probably about twelve guys.

I had the "opportunity" to stand bridge watches when I was on the *Reeves*. I was a third class and on my second deployment with her. First division happened to be shorthanded, and since the Second Division (gunner's mates and fire controlmen) was part of the weapons department, we got recruited to stand bridge watches underway to fill in for the shortage of bos'n's mates.

I was a petty officer third class at the time, so I was assigned to stand bos'n's mate of the watch. I was in charge of the watch section and had to make sure everyone got rotated on time. I had to check running lights at night and report to the officer of the deck that they were lit hourly. I had to pass the word over the ship's intercom as required and just, in general, be available to the officer of the deck at all times.

I hated having to stand bridge watches, and I resented being called a bos'n's mate. No offense to bos'n's mates—it's just that I worked hard to become a gunner's mate. Whenever I'd relieve the guy before me, I'd go up to the officer of the deck to report that I'd assumed the watch. I'd report, "Officer of the deck, I've assumed the duties as gunner's mate of the watch, sir."

Some of the officers were cool with it, but a couple weren't and would make me say it again properly. Anal little shits.

## Heavy Seas

Riding a destroyer was awesome. When the seas were calm, the ship rolled and pitched with a pretty gentle motion. You hardly noticed there was any movement at all. The sunsets and sunrises were breathtaking and could give a person such a sense of peace and tranquility. When the seas were rough, it could be like a roller-coaster ride—exciting but scary at the same time. I've been through a lot of storms out there, seen blue water come over the bridge, and taken thirty-degree rolls.

In conditions like that, any topside spaces were off-limits, the ship's buttoned up pretty tight, and all you could do was hang on and ride it out. Some of the worst storms I saw were in the Sea of Japan, but I've seen them all over the Pacific and Indian Ocean.

When the swells got big—twenty to thirty feet high—destroyers rode a little rough. As the ship rode up the front or back of a swell, it was like climbing a hill. Once it reached the peak of the swell and crests, it started down the other side so you were going downhill. When it reached the bottom of the swell and buried the bow, the ship shuddered, then started back up, all the time rolling left and right, sometimes a lot.

Often, the officer of the deck would alter course, so the ship rode into the swells, but that wasn't always an option. Sometimes the ship had to ride "the trough," so the swells came into the ship from the side. This is called riding the trough. We used to joke about it being the "supper course" because it always seemed to happen at mealtime. It made it miserable to try to eat.

Regardless of heavy seas, destroyer life went on as normally as possible, even movie call. I remember a few times when a couple shipmates had to sit on either side of the movie projector and hold on to it so we could watch the movie. Pretty much the only things that changed during heavy seas was that topside was secured and meals were simple because they couldn't cook. A lot of times, we'd be watching the movie, and all of a sudden, there'd be a loud long crash coming from the galley because the cooks didn't secure the pans well enough. Everything on a destroyer had to be well tied down, or it'd get loose and possibly hurt someone or, at the very least, cause damage and a lot of noise.

## Gunnery

Naval gunnery is a very complex operation. You're firing from a moving platform, at a moving target, whether it's in the air or on the surface. The only exception is shore bombardment, but even then, with the ships in motion, it can be pretty challenging. As a gunner's mate, it's very rewarding and exciting. Out of all the different ratings I could have gone into, I'm glad I chose it. It was dangerous but exciting. I worked on 3"/50, 5"/54, and 76 mm rapid-fire guns. All of them were awesome, but my favorite were the five-inch guns.

All the guns have different operating modes. If you're shooting at a fast-moving air target, the gun is actually aimed by a fire control director, which has the target on radar. The speed of the ship, the speed of the target, the lead angle, the ship's course, the target's course, and the wind speed are all fed into a computer for a final fire control solution. The gun is switched into auto mode, matches up with the director, and if all is right, you hit the target. The same is true for surface targets.

Another mode of operation is the local surface mode. The guns have optical sights and hand controls so the operator can look through the sight and control the elevation and train of the gun mount to keep it on target. He also has a firing key so he can fire the gun when he's on target. This mode of operation is used if the fire control director is inoperable or also to fire at surface targets. Ships have to "qualify" yearly in all modes of operation to make sure they can "hit the target." I loved the qualifying exercises. We *always* excelled.

The targets we shot at were very hard to see with the naked eye. If it was an air shoot, a plane would fly over with an orange sleeve trailing behind on a cable, probably about one hundred yards behind the airplane. We had to use an "offset" of about five mils behind the sleeve. We used variable time fragmentation rounds for those exercises. The rounds would explode when they got within close proximity to the target. If you watched, you'd see a tiny orange sleeve, followed by a bunch of puffs of smoke.

Surface targets were a small, orange sled towed by another ship on a cable about five hundred yards behind the ship. Again, we had to use a five-mil offset so we wouldn't destroy the target. I remember my first local surface gunshot as a mount captain. I had to spot the rounds and make corrections to the sight setter. Nobody told me I was supposed to use an offset, so I made corrections to hit the target. Within five rounds, I was hitting the target sled and blew the shit out of it.

Once I hit it, I went to rapid-fire and got off about six rounds before I heard over the phones, "Mount 31, cease fire, cease fire."

Then they told me I wasn't supposed to actually "hit" the target but lead five mils behind it. I blew the shit out of that target sled though. My chief thought it was funny and slapped me on the back. I didn't get in any trouble, but I heard the tug's captain that was towing it was pretty *pissed*.

We also used other things as targets. We had these large inflatable targets that when inflated were probably fifteen feet across. They were bright orange, and we'd tie them to five-gallon cans full of water to keep them in place. We'd drop them over the side, then the ship would back off about five to ten thousand yards, then we'd do some target practice. I never saw one of those targets come back aboard intact. We also used fifty-five-gallon drums to shoot at. Those, we always sank.

One last thing about firing at surface targets in local surface mode. The ship pitches and rolls. It's pretty easy to keep the sight crosshairs on a target, but the timing of when you pull the trigger is very important. If you fire when the ship rolls left one minute, then you fire when the ship rolls right the next, there's going to be a huge difference where the rounds land, hundreds of yards' difference. The rule of thumb was to always fire at the peak of the up roll.

Whenever a gun mount is going to be fired, a "prefire" checklist has to be completed. There are certain things that have to be checked to ensure the gun fires safely. The firing circuit has to be checked. This is done by placing a primer cartridge into a specially modified shell casing, inserting in the breach, then closing the firing key. If it pops, the firing circuit is okay; if it doesn't, the gunners need to figure out why. This is done to make sure that when an actual live round is chambered and the firing key is closed, you won't have a "misfire."

Misfires are bad on a big gun because the projectiles are highly explosive, and you don't want them to be in the barrel too long, especially if you've been firing for a while and the barrel is hot. The heat from the barrel can cause the projectile to explode.

(A funny story here. When I was in Vietnam, and we were doing prefires every day, I loaded up the primers on one of the guns, squeezed the firing key, and a shitload of marijuana blew out of the barrel and scattered everywhere. Apparently, someone had chosen the gun barrel muzzle to hide their stash. Not a very smart move.)

Another thing that has to be checked is the recoil and counter-recoil fluid. When the gun fires, recoil fluid is what buffers the recoil of the gun. If there isn't enough fluid, the gun can slam back and cause some pretty severe damage, possibly kill the gun crew. Train and elevation have to be checked to make sure the gun mount responds properly. A bore plug gauge has to be passed down the barrel to make sure there aren't any obstructions in the barrel. Dummy rounds have to be cycled through the loading system. Transmission checks have to be conducted to make sure the gun aligns with and follows the fire control director.

Fire hoses have to be laid out nearby in case of a misfire in a hot gun. The fire hoses are used to cool the barrel. Lubrication of the breach has to be checked to make sure it doesn't hang up when it opens and closes. There are numerous other things that have to be checked, but I can't remember them all.

Once all the checks are done, the checklist has to be signed by the gunnery officer, then taken to the captain. Whenever you're in a combat zone, it has to be done every morning. We had to do it when I was in Vietnam, then again years later in the Persian Gulf.

A smooth gunnery exercise was always a blessing—and what we strived for—but there was always the chance that something could go wrong despite all the safety checks. Machines break down from time to time, and gun mounts are machines. My first encounter was when I was a loader on the three-inch mounts on my first ship.

We were doing an air shoot, the target was making its third pass, so we'd fired about thirty rounds already. We opened fire, and the empty shell casing from the second round on my loader jumped out of the empty case chute and blocked the chute, so all the empty shell cases started piling up. The gun was elevating, and I knew that if I didn't get those empty shell cases out of there, we'd have a serious problem, but I didn't want to stop the firing exercise. Being the stupid young guy that I was, I reached down and grabbed one to clear it.

The empty shell cases were *hot*. They'd just been heated to over a thousand degrees. My left palm was instantly blistered. I didn't hold on to that shell casing very long. I yelled to Dave, who was the mount captain, and he shut the gun mount down. I ended up going down to sick bay, and the rest of the exercise was canceled.

During another shoot, I was the sight setter during a surface shoot. I stood behind the local surface operator who was controlling the gun mount. He would fire a round; the mount captain would give me the corrections; and I'd crank them in and then tap the head of the local surface operator to let him know I was done so he could fire. At one point, I guess I tapped his head a little hard because he flinched, and when he did, he suddenly depressed the gun barrel and fired at the same time. The round went into the water about thirty feet away from the ship. After that we stopped using the tapping system. I would just speak into my phones, "Sight set."

Another time, when I was on five-inch guns, we were doing naval gunfire support qualifications. I was the mount captain.

We'd been firing all day and were well within the "hot gun" zone. We were doing a ten-round salvo when, all of a sudden, the gun stopped firing and the safety observer in the gun mount called down on my phones, "Foul bore, foul bore!" Not something you want to hear when you have a hot gun. I called back up to him and asked him if he could see the cause. He couldn't. He did tell me that the breach block was partway open. That just made the situation even worse. If the round went off, the explosion could travel out of the breach and into the gun mount.

When you have a foul bore in a hot gun, you have a limited time to get it clear before the heat "cooks off" the high explosive round. If I remember right, when I got the foul bore report, I looked at the chart, which was on the control panel in front of me, and it said we had eight minutes to clear the round. We used up about four minutes with the safety observer trying to figure out what happened. I reported everything to gun control and was told to aim the gun at a safe firing bearing and evacuate the gun mount carrier room and magazine, which I did. Then my chief and I ran up to the gun to see what we could do. The bridge yelled down at us with a bullhorn to evacuate, but we climbed into the gun mount instead. It only took us a minute to find that a nut had backed off the breach operating rod. We grabbed some pliers, yanked up on the operating rod, and she "fired." The bore was clear, the gun mount was saved, and nobody got killed, but the chief and I were in some pretty hot water with the captain. I've had my ass chewed before, but nothing compared to that one. We had disobeyed the captain's direct order.

I think back about that from time to time, and I truly believe in my heart that the reason we didn't receive any punishment other than an ass chewing was because the captain was secretly glad that we'd done what we did. If we hadn't, the projectile would have eventually detonated and, at the very least, would have blown the barrel. At the worst, the explosion would have traveled out of the breech and down into the carrier room. I've been through firing exercises where we fired so many rounds that the paint on the barrel would blister, peel, and burn.

One time I was the mount captain. We were doing a firing exercise, and in the middle of a salvo, I heard a loud bang, which wasn't a round being fired. The safety observer in the mount called down and said there was a live round in the gun pocket that had jumped out of a transfer tray. I called gun control and told them I had a casualty and had to shut down. I shut down and climbed up into the gun pocket, and sure enough, there was a live round and full powder case lying at the bottom of the pocket. They had fallen about ten feet from the gun slide-and-transfer tray. I yelled down to one of my gun crew, grabbed the seventy-eight-pound projectile, and passed it down to him.

I yelled down, "Get it up and over the side, quick!"

He did. I've never seen anyone run so fast carrying seventy-eight pounds. I wasn't too worried about the powder can though. The only way it would have gone off was if the primer was hit with an electric charge. As it turned out, a linkage that opened and closed the transfer tray had snapped. All the preventive maintenance in the world couldn't have prevented it.

When I was still on three-inch guns, we were doing a firing exercise, and in the middle of it, I ended up with a misfire. I took the gun to a safe firing bearing and was concentrating on trying to get it clear. We still had a cold gun, so there wasn't a huge rush. It took about five minutes for me to figure out why. While I was preoccupied, one of my ammo passers, a new guy, had wandered around to the front of the gun mount and was fucking around with the empty shell cases. I didn't know it. When I got the problem fixed, I got permission to fire and happened to look up just as I squeezed the firing key. The gun fired, and I saw a person hit the deck. The blast from the barrel knocked him down. He got up and ran aft. He wasn't hurt, just a little shaken up. He got reassigned to another general quarters station after that.

It wasn't just the gun mounts that would give you problems. I was firing a .50caliber machine gun once and had it jam up on me. I tried to jack the breech back, but it wouldn't budge. I opened the cover and discovered that the breech wasn't all the way forward, and there was a round chambered. For the life of me, I couldn't get the damn thing to jack out of there. I ended up getting a long rod and hammer, and with a little help from one of the other gunners, I managed to tap the round out by sticking the rod down the barrel and tapping on it with a hammer while he pulled back on the charging handle. We got it out, but what we found was that when a previous round had fired, and the extractors pulled the empty case out of the chamber, it pulled the base of the shell casing off, and the rest of the casing was still in the chamber. When the next round chambered, it lodged into that empty case. We checked the headspace and timing, and it was spot-on. The only thing I could figure was that the round was faulty.

Ammunition for the guns is another thing the gunners are responsible for. A Knox-class frigate has two magazines below the gun mount and carrier room. They're fairly large compartments and can hold several hundred rounds of ammunition. There's a magazine for powder cans and a separate one for projectiles.

The projectiles are stowed in racks and separated by type, high explosive frag, mechanical time fuse, variable time fuse, white phosphorous, etc.

The powder cans are stowed in racks, but there are no different types of powder cans—they're all the same. But they are shipped and stored in aluminum containers to keep from damaging the primer and to keep them dry. The only different types of powder cans a ship carries are about a half dozen "short" charges. These are powder cans that are about half the length of a regular can and are used in the event of a foul bore to expel the projectile out of the barrel.

During normal operations, a ship carries a full complement of ammunition. If the ammunition becomes depleted due to gunnery training or combat, the ship has to replenish it. Going to the ammo piers was never a fun thing for us gunners. We had to rig the ammunition hoist in a trunk that went from the main deck down to the magazine. It was a type of elevator that held about sixteen projectiles at a time; it was raised and lowered with an air hoist controlled by a pendant.

The ammunition was lifted by crane from the pier to the foc'sle, then a couple guys would lift them by hand and set them into the hoist. The hoist was lowered down to the magazine, where it was unloaded by hand and stacked in the bins. The hoist was raised back up, and the whole thing was repeated. Once the projectiles were loaded, we had to set the elevator up for powder cans and repeat the entire process. Ammunition onloads could last all day. It was not a fast process, and it always wore everyone out.

Believe me, lifting seventy-eight-pound projectiles all day is a bitch. Also, as we stacked the projectile in the bins, we had to lift them higher and higher as the bins filled up. The last few rows, which were almost to the overhead, were the worst because we had to basically lift them over our heads. All in all, it took about twenty men to load ammo.

Whenever a ship goes into the shipyards for overhaul, all the ammunition has to be off-loaded. Once a ship completes overhaul, all the ammunition has to be onloaded. Those two instances are pretty miserable if you're a gunner. Also, one other thing that sucked was that while a ship was at the ammunition depot, the smoking lamp was "out."

## Horseplay

New crew members, the ones fresh out of boot camp or A school, *always* got fucked with by the "salts" (seasoned sailors). It was fun and was meant in good spirits. It was a way to teach them to think for themselves and gain some nautical wisdom and humility.

Anyone who's served aboard ship knows about "sea bats." This one takes the coordination of several sailors. You get a small cardboard box, poke a bunch of holes in it, place it on a bit, then a couple sailors lean over it, peeking in the top, oohing and aahing, while a couple more sailors stand by with brooms, pretending to sweep the deck. New guy comes along, gets curious, asks what it is, sailors say, "It's a sea bat." New guy wants to see, bends over to look in the box, gets his ass hit with a broom. Everybody laughs, even the new guy.

Then there's the search for nonexistent items. The entire ship is in on this one. A new guy gets sent from space to space looking for something he was sent to find. Of course, nobody has it and sends him elsewhere. I've seen guys get sent down to the fireroom for a bucket of steam, to the bos'n locker for six fathoms of water line or shoreline, to the bos'n locker for nonskid polish, and all over for relative-bearing grease. They always ultimately catch on, but sometimes it takes a while.

We had one kid spend about four hours going around asking for relative-bearing grease. He got sent to the bos'n locker, the engine room, the fireroom, the HT shop, the galley, the laundry, the ET shop, the signal shack, the torpedomen, the gunner's mates, even the bridge. He still came back empty-handed.

Mail buoy watch—this is a good one. The new guy gets told that he has the mail buoy watch. He's told to get a set of sound-powered phones and go up to the ship's bow, make comms with the bridge, and watch for the mail buoy. Of course, the entire bridge watch section is in on it, even the officer of the deck. I've seen guys stand up there for four hours, until they're told to secure by the bridge phone talker. We even had a couple that reported contacts that they thought might be the mail buoy.

B1RDs. The new guy is standing after lookout watch. His job is to report any contacts, air or surface, to the bridge. Salts are standing around on the fantail. One of them goes over to the aft lookout and asks him if he reported the B1RD to the bridge.

New guy says, "What's B1RD?"

Salt says, "That one out there," pointing aft.

New guy says, "I don't see anything."

Salt says, "It's right out there, about 185 degrees, position angle 2! About ten thousand yards. Don't you see it?"

The new guy can't see it, of course, but trusts the salt. He calls up to the bridge phone talker.

"Bridge, aft look out. I have a B1RD at 185 degrees, position angle 2, approximately ten thousand yards."

Of course, the bridge phone talker, who must relay everything to the officer of the deck, announces that the aft lookout reports a B1RD at 185 degrees, position angle 2, and approximately ten thousand yards. The entire bridge watch section laughs, including the officer of the deck and the captain (if he's present). The bridge phone talker calls back down to the aft lookout to disregard the B1RD—it's only a bird, probably a seagull.

This isn't necessarily "horseplay," but one of the major leisure time activities aboard a destroyer is "fishing." I've spent countless hours, along with my shipmates, back on the fantail with my line in the water. Any time after knock-off, and the ship was moving slow, there'd be about a dozen sailors back on the fantail with lines in the water, "trolling."

None of us really knew what we were fishing for, but whatever took the hook was fun. The galley wouldn't let us cook them, but they were fun to catch. The only exception was that we could set up a barbecue on the flight deck and barbecue what we caught. The only time we did was whenever someone would catch something big or a bunch of smaller fish. We did catch a lot of tuna, which was wonderful when grilled.

My gunner's mate first class brought up a six-foot-long barracuda once. One time I was using a deep-sea rig with about a three-inch hook on a steel leader. I baited it with a six-inch-long fish that someone else had caught, had the line out about a hundred feet from the ship, and something took the hook. Whatever it was, it was big. I could hardly get any headway reeling it in. I fought that thing for about thirty minutes; everyone else pulled their lines in and just watched. All of a sudden, my line went slack, so I started reeling it in. When I finally got my line in, the steel leader was cut off and the hook was gone. To this day, I believe it was a very large shark.

Some guys even brought up small sharks. The biggest I can remember was about three feet long. We had one guy even pull up a sea snake once, which didn't go over too well with the executive officer. He happened to walk back to the fantail and caught about six guys standing around this live sea snake that was crawling around on the deck. He flipped out. If I remember right, we lost our fishing privileges for about two weeks over that one.

We also had volleyball games on the flight deck. We never used real volleyballs because they wouldn't last long. One bad play and it was over the side. We'd wad up paper into a ball, wrap it with masking tape, then play until it went over the side, then make another one. I wonder sometimes how many of those balls actually washed ashore somewhere and what anyone thought if they found them.

Steel Beach picnics were a nice break in the routine. We'd drag out the barbecues, and the cooks would grill steak or hamburgers and hotdogs. Everyone would sit on the flight deck to eat and just relax. Sometimes it's the little things that can make a huge difference in morale.

Occasionally, we'd have a casino night on the messdecks. We had roulette wheels, dice, and cards. You could buy chips and gamble, even though gambling is against the rules. They set betting limits, and it was just a fun evening. They even put out snacks and beverages. By the way, roulette wheels work a little differently when the ship rolls and pitches. As they say, "It's a gamble." That's another reason why they don't have pool tables on ships.

Whenever a ship is away from her homeport for a couple weeks or longer, the night before pulling back in is almost always channel fever night. Everyone is anxious to see their families again, and it's hard to sleep anticipating returning home. They show movies all night on the messdecks, often set out snacks for everyone, and there's an air of excitement throughout the ship. I always enjoyed it, but I enjoyed pulling into our home port the next day even more.

# CHAPTER FIVE

# Liberty Call

Liberty call—music to a sailor's ears. A chance to get off the ship and explore and have fun. Liberty in your home port is great, but liberty overseas is an adventure. The great thing about being on a destroyer is that you get to pull into ports that the bigger ships can't. Sometimes that isn't such a blessing—there are some real shitholes over there. Somalia comes to mind.

On deployment, a ship will pull into a liberty port about every four to six weeks, sometimes more, sometimes less. It's hard to describe the feeling of going ashore in a foreign port after being confined for that long. *Exhilaration* would be one word for it. "Join the navy and see the world," used to be a recruiting slogan. Yep, if you're on a destroyer, you do—sometimes more of the world than you want to see. But mostly, you see the ocean.

My first foreign liberty port was Olongapo City in the Philippines. I already talked a little about it, but there's a lot more to it than just bars. Outside of Olongapo, there's Subic City, just about a fifteen-minute jeepney ride. It's a small town made up mostly of bars. Everything was cheaper there and was well worth the trip. It wasn't as crowded as Olongapo either. My favorite place in Subic City was "Marilyn's," just a small, quiet bar.

I was sitting at the bar one time, and a young Filipino guy came in, walked up to me, and said, "Hey, Joe, you want a tattoo?"

I told him I wasn't looking to get a tattoo. I just wanted to sit where I was and drink my beer.

He said, "No problem, Joe. I do right here."

I asked him how he was going to do that, and he unrolled a cloth on the bar with a bunch of bamboo needles and said, "With this."

I was kind of intrigued, so I sketched a heart on a bar napkin, with my two daughters' names in it, and told him, "Go ahead."

I had him do it on my left shoulder, and it actually turned out pretty good. It took a little getting used to being jabbed with bamboo needles, but the beer helped. He was pretty quick and only charged me twenty pesos, which was about two American dollars. I decided to have him do another one on my back. He did a Pegasus on my right shoulder blade, about five inches across. It took him a lot longer, but I think he did a pretty good job. He charged me forty pesos, which I thought was fair, and he went on his way. I went back to the ship that night, a little inebriated, and didn't think much more about it.

The next morning, I climbed out of my rack, went into the head to take a shower, and one of my shipmates asked me, "Hey, Sams, what's that on your back? It looks like a pizza."

I looked in the mirror as best I could, and it *did* look like a pizza, or at least a blob. As it turned out though, it was just swollen and red. As it healed, it looked like it was supposed to. It had me worried though. I also worried about infection or getting some kind of disease from dirty needles. A person does some stupid things when they've been drinking. But everything turned out fine. It was a life experience I wouldn't trade for anything.

On the way to Subic City, there's a resort called White Rock. You can rent a room that gives out onto the beach. They also had a huge swimming pool with a high dive platform. A really relaxing place. I spent considerable time there.

Hong Kong was pretty cool. A little expensive, but it was an interesting place. The food was wonderful. I've never had Chinese food that even compares to Hong Kong. It was a big place, crowded, and it was easy to get lost.

Singapore was awesome. One of the cleanest ports I've ever been in. No litter anywhere in the city. The captain imposed a dress code for the crew going ashore. We had to wear shirts with collars, slacks, and no tennis shoes. It was a pretty civilized place. They even had an A&W Root Beer restaurant and a Pizza Hut. I stopped at the A&W and ordered a hamburger, sat down to eat it, took one bite (which tasted like shit), found something rubbery in the bite, spit it out, and there in the bite was a piece of an artery. I threw it away, ate the fries, and left. The Tiger Balm Gardens were worth visiting. It's a sort of park with a bunch of displays made up of plaster figures depicting all kinds of things from Singapore's religious culture, very colorful and in some cases kind of gruesome. Souvenir shopping was pretty good but kind of expensive. I always did a lot of shopping overseas, gifts for everyone back home. Public drunkenness is forbidden. They had bars and nightclubs, but you really had to watch how much you drank.

Taiwan was a crazy place. It was very crowded and kind of dirty, with lots of bars and hookers. Great for shopping though. Apparently, Taiwan didn't believe in copyrights. I've never seen so many record shops and bookstores. You could buy any record album or book you can imagine, dirt cheap. The only problem with the record albums was that about the fourth time you played them, they'd start skipping. Not really a bargain. The books were okay though, if you didn't mind missing chapters or sections.

Surabaya, Indonesia, was pretty memorable. The public pier where we tied up would flood when the tide came in at night. If you were returning to the ship from liberty, you had to wade through about an inch of water. Rats—they were everywhere and the biggest rats I've ever seen. The town stank. We could smell it even before we got to the pier. Out in town, sewage ran through open ditches along the roads. There were whorehouses everywhere, if you wanted to take a chance. Overall, not a place I'd like to see again.

Japan was pretty awesome. I got to visit Yokosuka and Sasebo. It was a pretty crowded place but civilized. It had lots of bars and nightclubs and a McDonald's restaurant that actually tasted right. There were lots of restaurants, and the food was great—you just had to be careful what you ordered. Some of the restaurants didn't have anyone that could speak English, and we certainly couldn't speak Japanese, so we would just point to something on the menu and hope for the best. One time I ended up with raw octopus. Kind of rubbery, but I choked it down.

I also had the opportunity to go snow skiing in Japan. We pulled into Yokosuka, and the naval base had special services where you could book tours and recreational activities. Myself and about three others from the ship booked a skiing trip that lasted about four days. We had to take a train to the ski resort, which took about five hours. Then when we got there, we stayed in a small resort. The rooms we stayed in were traditional Japanese. The table was about a foot high, we had to sit on the floor to eat, and the beds were just pads on the floor with a blanket. We had to leave our shoes out in the hallway, and all the doors slid sideways. Skiing was wonderful. Everyone was friendly, and it was one of my most memorable adventures. I'm glad I did it.

My first impression of Karachi, Pakistan wasn't very good. When we saw the dead camel floating in the harbor on our way in and the flies that started to swarm the ship, I thought, "Another shithole." But it turned out to be pretty decent. After we tied up and before they passed liberty call, money changers came on board to exchange money for us. I handed them about fifty US dollars, and they gave me a stack of rupees that would choke a horse. Our first stop was the US Embassy, where they had a canteen and "beer." We had a few, then went out to explore. I've already talked some about Karachi, but there's a lot more to it.

On the outskirts of Karachi, along the beach, you could rent "camels" to ride along the beach. A couple of buddies of mine and I did just that. *Camels suck.* If you ever have the same opportunity, *don't do it.* As soon as I got on the camel and it stood up, all it wanted to do was bite me. It kept turning its head from left to right, trying to bite my legs. It didn't want to walk. It took the camel herder to coax it into finally walking down the beach. After we went maybe a quarter mile and decided to turn back, that camel took off on a dead run and wouldn't slow down until we got back to the herder, we rented them from. The camel and I did not make friends. And just as a sidenote—they spit at you.

I've been to Karachi a few times. On another trip there, we rented some horses to ride along the beach. That was a lot better than the camels. At least the horses would respond to you and were easier to control. Overall, it was an enjoyable day. Never again will I ride a camel!

Shopping in Karachi was fantastic. There was a street that consisted of a bunch of shops, open in the front, where they made and sold all kinds of handcrafted wooden tables, chairs, jewelry boxes, you name it. They were all made of beautiful hardwood, and they were all inlaid with copper and brass. They were absolutely beautiful. Some of the shops sold onyx lamps, goblets, ashtrays, and carved figurines. Other shops had just about everything you could think of engraved and made out of brass, figurines, tea sets, plates, and vases. The best part about it was everything was *cheap*. I did quite a bit of shopping in Karachi.

For a very small fee, you could rent an open horse-drawn carriage to tour the city. A couple of friends and I did that, and it was well worth the money.

Also, while we were there, the marine detachment for the US Embassy invited our crew to their compound for a party and a cookout. That was a very memorable day and evening. I ate so much, and since there wasn't anywhere in town where you could drink, I had a few with the marines. I made some friends and some memories. Semper fi, my brothers-in-arms. We had a good time, and I think of you guys often.

Ceylon / Sri Lanka wasn't very impressive. There wasn't much to do there except drink. Shopping wasn't very good; the only thing they had were gemstones. That seemed to be the big attraction. Guys were buying a lot of rubies, emeralds, and diamonds. I didn't trust them, so I stayed clear. The most memorable thing I can remember about Ceylon was hooking up with a couple British merchant sailors. We had a great time—man, those guys could drink. We wandered all over town, hitting the bars, and ended up back on their ship. They had a bar on their ship. The US Navy is the only navy that doesn't allow alcohol on board.

Mombasa, Kenya, was quite an adventure. We pulled in and had to anchor out, so we had to go ashore on the motor whale boat. Once onshore, it was *different*. The first place my buddies and I went to was the Elephant Bar. We walked in to get a cold beer, and it was *hot* in there. No air-conditioning, just overhead fans. We sat down at a table, ordered our beer, and when they brought it to us, it was room temperature. When you haven't had a beer in a while, even warm beer tastes good. It wasn't long till we were joined by several "bar girls." The best way I can describe them is *smelly*. I finished my beer as quickly as I could, then told my buddies I'd catch up to them later and left. Even though it was hot outside, the fresh air was good.

I walked down the main street of Mombasa, just taking it all in, and what did I see? *Kentucky Fried Chicken!* I couldn't believe it. So, I had to stop there. Make no mistake—Kentucky Fried Chicken tastes a lot better in the States. Not sure if it was even chicken. Another disappointment.

Some of the crew went on "safaris." They were "photography safaris." I wanted to go but couldn't afford it. Now I wish I had.

Souvenir shopping was pretty awesome. They had all kinds of wood carvings for sale. All African art—carved elephants, gazelles, giraffes, masks, and lions. I was bartering with a vendor for a carved elephant, and he pointed at my watch, which was a cheap digital Timex I probably spent six dollars on, and he said, "Trade." He wanted to trade the elephant for my watch. Of course, I "traded."

Then I was looking at another carving, and the guy pointed at my shirt and said, "Trade."

I declined. I needed my shirt to get back on board the ship, but it gave me an idea. I went back to the ship, opened my locker, and dug out all the clothes I didn't wear anymore. I headed back up to the quarterdeck with an armload of clothes, and the officer of the deck asked me where I was going with them. So I explained to him that I was taking them ashore to "trade."

Before I knew it, the OOD, petty officer of the watch, and command duty officer all had old clothes to trade. I suddenly had bags of clothes to take ashore to trade for souvenirs. The upside was that the CDO had the captain's gig take me back to shore, then waited for me to do the "trading."

The vendors were "all about" the clothing. It was more valuable than money. I probably made eight trips from the marketplace to the captain's gig carrying wood carvings. When I finally got back on board, I distributed the souvenirs to everyone who'd donated, and everyone was happy. I brought back a bunch of souvenirs from Mombasa.

Mauritius is an island off the east coast of Africa. Not much of a "drinking" port, but it was interesting all the same. It was kind of a dull place, but sightseeing was okay. The high point for me was that the ship asked for volunteers to help rebuild a rural schoolhouse. I volunteered. They took about sixteen of us out to the village outside of town. The school was made out of adobe, I guess. It had a tin roof and two classrooms.

When we got there, there were kids everywhere. We met with the teacher then started repairing the place, cleaning and painting it. The ship even donated a bunch of supplies like paper, pencils, chalk, erasers, and all kinds of stuff.

What was so great about it was that the kids, all barefoot and wearing rags, were in there helping us. We didn't speak the same language, but it didn't matter. We worked and played with those kids, and it left a warm place in my heart. I was glad we could make a difference in their lives.

At lunchtime, the ship sent us all boxed lunches. A couple of sandwiches, a boiled egg, a couple of cookies, and potato chips. The schoolmaster asked us to close the shutters and doors while we ate our lunch. All the kids were outside. We started eating our lunch, but it didn't seem right to me. I wasn't very hungry, so I opened one of the shutters, and all the kids were standing right outside.

I gave half a sandwich to the closest kid, and oh my god, he took off running with a bunch of kids chasing him. Then I realized, along with the rest of my shipmates, that these kids were starving. We had some extra boxed lunches, and everyone started passing out food to the kids. They went nuts. It really broke my heart. After we passed out all the food, I walked up to a little country store about a quarter mile away, bought all the candy they had, took it back to the school, and passed it out to all the kids. I've never seen kids so happy. It stays with me to this day.

Somalia is not a hospitable place. I wrote before about the Somali guard who was ready to shoot me. The people there weren't very friendly. Of course, if I lived like they did, I probably wouldn't be very friendly either. There was *nothing* there. It was dry, desolate, dirty. The people were starving, lived in mud huts, and had absolutely nothing going for them.

One of the things I noticed while we were there (I don't remember if it was Djibouti or Berbera) was that at the port there were open pole buildings *full* of rice or wheat (I wasn't sure what). But the sacks were all stenciled with "Care USA." There were people outside the port who were starving, but all the food donated by the US was sitting in those pole buildings. Somalia was a pretty corrupt and unstable place. By the way, all the people I saw in Somalia were skin and bones.

Bahrain was a relief to visit. We tied up there after about three months at sea in the Persian Gulf. I can honestly say that I've never been so tired of being at sea. We were only there for three days, but it was a welcome respite. The first place my buddies and I went was the American Service Unit. It's a small US military base. They had an enlisted men's club and a chief's club. Boy did that beer taste good. There wasn't much else to do there other than sightsee and shop.

We went to the marketplace in town. I've never seen so much gold in my life. What a contrast to places like Pakistan. There were jewelry and perfume shops everywhere, and the displays of gold in the windows were incredible. It was hard to imagine that they could display so much gold and not get robbed, but then the laws were a lot stricter there and the punishments more severe. The gold was relatively low-priced and a bargain. There were several high-class hotels there that had lounges and sold alcohol, but public drunkenness was forbidden, so what drinking we did was at the American Service Unit.

By far, my favorite liberty was Australia. I had the pleasure of visiting three different ports there. The first was Albany, at the southern tip of Australia's west coast. The other two were Melbourne and Sydney on the east coast.

Albany was fantastic. The people there were very hospitable and friendly. As a matter of fact, we pulled in on a Sunday, and businesses in town that were normally closed on Sunday opened up. Half the town was standing on the pier to welcome us when we tied up. It was amazing. There were several bars in town, and it seemed that everyone wanted to buy us a drink and talk to us. It was hard to buy a drink for yourself. Some of my fellow first-class petty officers and myself rented a motel room behind one of the bars, bought cases of beer, and used the room as a home base while we were there.

The first night there, I guess we got a little loud, and someone called the police on us. The police came knocking at the door to investigate and ended up drinking with us until the wee hours. Every night we were there, so were the police, even if they were on duty. They were some pretty cool guys. In fact, the morning we left, they gave us a ride back to the ship in their police cars. They even made us all honorary Albany policemen.

A lot of the citizens came to the ship and left invitations for us for different things, like parties or outings. I accepted one from a family that wanted a sailor to go with them sightseeing along the coast and a picnic. It was a lady named Ann and her two sons, about eight and ten years old. It was great. I got to see some beautiful scenery, ate an awesome picnic lunch, made some friends, and just had a fantastic time. At the end of the day, I invited them aboard the ship, gave them a tour, and had them join me for supper on the messdecks. They loved it.

I also had the opportunity to go on a guided horseback ride along the cliffs overlooking the ocean. It was very memorable.

I saw some beautiful scenery, even saw kangaroos, took a lot of pictures, and made more friends. The people in Albany were just awesome.

Melbourne and Sydney were pretty cool, but a little more reserved than Albany. The people were friendly, but not as much as Albany. Melbourne was beautiful. We were there during their autumn. The leaves were all changing color, and it made me a little homesick. I did get to visit the Sydney Opera House, which was pretty impressive.

I have to say though, out of all the ports I visited, there was still *no place like home.* The best part of all my deployments was *coming home.* I was married during three of my deployments, and I can tell you, I missed my wife and children tremendously. Six or seven months is a long time to be away from your family. You worry constantly if they're safe and okay. When you return home, your kids have grown, and you've missed out on a piece of their lives that you can't get back. Even your relationship with your spouse is different, and you have to get reacquainted with each other. Being a married navy man is not an easy thing. Leaving on deployment was always one of the hardest things I ever had to do.

# Chapter Six

# Old Friends

It always amazed me just how small the navy community really is. Throughout my career, I was constantly running into people with whom I'd been stationed in the past. I've already mentioned Master Chief Surdez, Master Chief Evans, and Dave, but there were many more times that it happened.

When I was a chief on the *Rathburne*, we were moored at Bravo piers in Pearl Harbor. I had duty this one day, as duty weapons officer, and was given the word that we needed to assemble line handlers because the USS *Whipple* was coming into port and was to moor outboard of us. When the time came and the *Whipple* was coming alongside, there on her fantail was Darryl Williams. Darryl had been my neighbor when I was stationed as an instructor in Great Lakes. We used to sit out in the yard in the summertime and drink beer and Mojo. He was a chief now as I was.

"I guess they let just about anybody into this port nowadays!" I yelled at him.

He looked at me and said, "I'll be damned, Kenny! By the way, I still have that hammer I borrowed from you years ago!"

I said, "I still have that bar and barstools I bought from you years ago!"

We laughed, and after the brow was over, he came over and had coffee with me, and we got caught up on the last few years.

We ended up getting together quite a bit after that, either at his house or mine. I even ended up with my hammer back and ended up selling him his bar back, which he regretted selling in the first place.

Another time, while I was on the *Rathburne*, I was standing a quarterdeck watch as officer of the deck. We had a ship tied up outboard of us (can't remember the name). A chief came off the outboard ship, stopped, and saluted me, as is the custom, and I went to salute back. And there stood Jack Kocher.

"I'll be dipped in shit!" I said.

"So will I!" he replied.

Jack had been a fellow instructor when I was at Great Lakes. We had been good friends and had spent a lot of time together back then. We ended up getting together again many times.

Back when I was an instructor at gunnery school, I was walking by the first deck classrooms. One of the C school classes was outside their classroom on a break. As I walked by, I noticed Ray Curtis standing there. Ray had been stationed with me on the *Reeves* when we were both seamen. We were together in Vietnam and had become best friends. Ray worked on mount 32, and I worked on mount 31.

He noticed me, broke out in a big smile, and said, "Damn, it's Ol' Ken Sams!"

That's what he always used to call me. We got together again and had more good times. He ended up getting stationed in Colts Neck, New Jersey, and I flew up to visit with him when I was going to school in Louisville, Kentucky. We've kept in touch off and on over the years. I consider him to be my closest navy brother.

One day when I was on the *Ouellet*, we were on deployment and had pulled into the Philippines. I was on liberty and walking down the main street, Magsaysay, when I heard someone behind me yelling, "Petty Officer Sams, Petty Officer Sams!"

I turned around to see this young man running up to me, *really excited.*

When he caught up to me, he said, "Remember me, Petty Officer Sams? You were my favorite instructor in A school!"

I remembered his face but couldn't remember his name. I taught a lot of classes when I was an instructor. He seemed disappointed that I couldn't remember his name, but when he told me, it all came back. We had a drink together; he seemed happy and satisfied with it. I was glad I could bring him some happiness.

After I left the navy, I got a job as a millwright for Alcoa, in Vancouver, Washington. They assigned me to graveyard shift. The leadman I worked for was named Bud. He seemed familiar, but I couldn't quite place him in my memory. We got along very well. He was an electrician, and I was a millwright (the mechanical side of industrial maintenance).

After about a month, we were sitting in the lunchroom, eating our lunch, and the topic turned to what we had done prior to Alcoa. I mentioned that I had been in the navy, and he said that he had too. So the conversation moved to where we had been and what ships we had been on. As it turned out, we had both been stationed on the *Meyerkord* at the same time. Then it hit me—he was Senior Chief Electrician's Mate Novak. I told him that when I was on the *Meyerkord*, I was a gunner's mate second class. He remembered me. We became good friends and even hunting partners.

I worked for another company after that. A machinery manufacturer, as the production supervisor. There was a guy there named Rick. He seemed familiar, but again, I couldn't quite place him in my memory. As it turned out, he had been stationed on the *Meyerkord* as an engineman at the same time as me. I remembered he used to maintain the engines on the captain's gig and the motor whaleboat. After we talked about it, it all came back to me who he was. Small world.

## Chief Surdez

The greatest man I've ever met was "Chief Surdez." He came aboard the *Reeves* in 1975. He was a chief gunner's mate and my division chief. I worked for many chiefs before but had never worked for a chief like him. Right away, after he reported aboard, my life changed. He was a chief who *truly* cared for his men. For some reason, he took a liking to me and became my "sea daddy." At the time, I was a gunner's mate third class. He was the most personable man I ever met and became an inspiration for me.

During my naval career, when faced with difficult decisions, I would often reflect, "What would Chief Surdez do?" especially when I became a chief myself.

Right away, he started calling me Boot Camp. He was always joking around with us and seemed to have a lot of respect for us, which made us respect him. He didn't demand respect like some chiefs did; he earned it and received it.

He had a serious side though. If we were in a gunnery exercise, he was all business and expected all of us to be the same. Prior to coming aboard the *Reeves*, he had served a couple tours in Vietnam on the airboats and riverboats. He was a pretty crusty guy.

I learned a lot about true leadership from him. I would have followed him to the ends of the earth.

He always had something funny to say. I remember him coming up to the gun mount, I'd be working on maintenance, and he'd say, "Goddamn, Boot Camp, you know what would do good right now?"

I'd say, "I don't know, Chief. What would?"

He'd say, "A fuck or a suck. Either get one or give one!"

The next day he'd come up to the gun mount and say, "Goddamn, Boot Camp. You know what would go good right now?"

I'd say, "A fuck or a suck, either get one or give one!"

He'd say, "No. A Baby Ruth candy bar!"

One day we were underway. I believe we were on deployment in the Indian Ocean. I was up working on the gun mount and had my navy-issue tennis shoes sitting on the gun mount because I had washed them and set them there to dry in the sun.

Chief Surdez came up to the gun mount, saw my shoes sitting there, and said, "What the fuck are these shoes doing on my gun mount?"

I said, "They're mine, Chief. I just put them there to dry."

He reached down, grabbed my shoes, and threw them over the side. I was awestruck. A few days later, I was up working on the gun mount, and Chief Surdez came up with a cup of coffee, in a cup called a "victory mug"—personalized, with his name on it—and set it down on the front of the gun mount. He was doing something on the back side of the gun.

I picked up his coffee cup and said, "What's this cup of coffee doing on my gun mount?" as I held it over the side.

He said, "You don't have the balls, Boot Camp!"

I let it drop. I thought he'd be pissed, but he just started laughing and said, "So you *do* have some balls," and slapped me on the back.

Another time, on the same deployment, it was *hot.* It gets pretty hot on a steel ship around the equator. It was just before payday. We were all flat broke, and none of us had a dime, which was what the ship's soda machine cost. We were up working on the gun mount in the heat, sweating our asses off, and Chief Surdez came up to see what we were doing.

He had his hand in his pocket and said, "Sure is fucking hot out here, isn't it?"

We were all, "Sure is, Chief!"

He started jingling a bunch of change in his pocket and said, "I bet you'd all like a nice, cold soda pop!"

Of course, we all said yes. He pulled out a handful of change, showed it to us, then immediately threw it over the side.

He said, "Fuck you, save some of your paycheck instead of drinking it up on liberty!"

He laughed and walked off. It was a lesson I learned, and I know to this day that it was intended by him to be a lesson. Of course, at the time, we were all dumbfounded. Sometimes lessons can be a little painful but will make a big impression.

We pulled into Yokosuka, Japan, that deployment. They passed liberty call, and I was lucky enough to have liberty the first night in. I and a couple other friends headed to the quarterdeck to leave the ship for a night on the town. This was the mid-'70s, so I was dressed as young men did during that time. I had a pair of saddle oxford shoes with thick heels on. Chief Surdez happened to be the officer of the deck on the quarterdeck.

As I got to the quarterdeck to leave the ship, Chief Surdez looked at me and said, "Goddamn, Boot Camp! Where are you going with those 'catch me, fuck me, hope I fall down, shoes?" Then he started laughing.

I went on liberty and had a good time, but I threw those shoes away.

Chief Surdez fucked with me all the time, but it was meant with good intent. He wouldn't have done it if he didn't care about me. I learned many good things from him—a lot of technical knowledge, a lot of job skills, but most importantly, humility, compassion, and a sense of humor.

Chief Surdez always had a joke to tell, almost every day. Some of them were really good, and some of them were pretty lame, but we always laughed at them. He always lightened our day.

He would come up with some of the most bizarre stuff.

One day he came up to me and said, "Hey, Boot Camp. You ever had a walk-off?"

Of course, I was curious to see where it was going, so I said, "No, Chief, never have. What's a walk-off?"

Then he told me, "Well, you take your clothes off, get in a tub of water, get a hard-on, then pour honey on the head of your pecker, when the flies land on it, they'll 'walk you off'!"

Another time, he came up and asked me if my wife ever used honey-flavored alum as a douche.

"No, Chief," I said.

He said, "Well, you should try it! It's sweeter to eat-er and teeter on the peter!" He laughed and walked off.

One day while we were on deployment, we had to test the magazine sprinkler systems. All the ammunition magazines on a ship are protected by an automatic sprinkling system that turns on either automatically or by a manual valve. It's designed to activate if there's high heat in the magazine, or it can be manually activated by a hand valve at either a remote location or in the magazine itself. These sprinkler systems spray seawater on the ammunition in case of a fire. Once a month, the gunner's mates have to test these systems to make sure they work if needed. In each magazine, there's a main valve that opens if there's a fire. To test the system, a "test casting" is installed in the main valve to divert the water from the sprinkler heads over the ammunition.

The test has to be conducted by the senior gunner's mate aboard. In this instance, it was Chief Surdez. He and I were down in the small arms magazine. We had installed the test casting and had a seaman who was new to our division manning the manual control valves, which were two decks up from where we were. I showed him what valve to turn. Everything was set.

Chief Surdez told me to yell up to Seaman Smith to turn the remote-control valve to "Open." I yelled up it for him. Nothing happened. Seaman Smith wasn't the most reliable individual and had a tendency to wander off, so we assumed that was what happened. After a couple minutes, I told Chief Surdez that I had better go check on him. I climbed up the two decks to the remote station, and there was Seaman Smith.

I told him, "I told you to go to 'Open.'"

He said, "I did."

I looked at the valve, which was labeled "3"/50 Magazine."

"Go to 'Close'!" I yelled.

He'd turned the wrong valve. I went back down to the small arms magazine and broke the news to Chief Surdez.

His only response was, "Shit."

We all climbed down to the three-inch magazine, which was three decks down a vertical ladder, to check the damage. We opened the last scuttle and looked down at about three feet of saltwater sloshing around. It was my turn to say, "Shit."

So we had two choices: either rig pumps to pump it out, which would alert everyone else to what happened and possibly get us in trouble, or we could empty it by hand with buckets tied to a rope. We all agreed to keep it as quiet as possible and do it by hand. That was probably the longest night of my life.

We worked all evening, all night, and part of the next morning hauling full buckets of water up three decks and emptying them in the division shower. Chief Surdez was right in there with the rest of us, lifting buckets up three decks. I really respected him for that. I know a lot of other chiefs that would have said, "Let me know when you're finished, I'll be in the chiefs' mess."

We all took turns, either passing buckets down in the magazine, hauling them up, or dumping them. Once we got all the salt water out, we weren't done yet. The 3"/50 rounds were in sealed aluminum canisters to protect them from moisture, but we still had to unstack all the ammo, wipe down the overhead and bulkheads with fresh water, then wipe all the ammo canisters with fresh water. Instead of hauling up salt water, we were hauling down clean fresh water.

All in all, I believe we spent about a week down there. After that, I hated going down into the magazine. Nobody outside our division ever found out about it until now, and I'm sure the statute of limitations has expired. Now it's just a sea story. It's too late to take us to captain's mast. By the way, we never had Seaman Smith help with sprinkler testing ever again!

Chief Surdez was never afraid to get his hands dirty. I remember so many times, working on one of the gun mounts, he'd come wandering up to check on us, and the next thing I knew, he was right in there helping.

One day I was on one of the guns painting—which you do a lot of aboard ship because of the corrosiveness of salt water. Chief Surdez came wandering by, stood watching me for a minute, then asked me if I had another paintbrush. I went into the gun shop, grabbed a brush, and handed it to him. It was really hot that day. We were out in the Indian Ocean, and I had my shirt off, so he took his off too and started painting along with me.

After about an hour, the captain came wandering by, stood there watching us for a few minutes, then he said to Chief Surdez, "Awful expensive painter, aren't you, Chief?"

Chief Surdez said to the captain, "Yes, sir, I guess I am that." He got off the gun mount, put his shirt back on as the captain wandered off, and I never saw him paint again.

Chief Surdez made senior chief while he was on board the *Reeves*. I ran into him a few years later in San Diego, and he was a master chief. It was when I was in the transient barracks on Coronado Amphibious Base waiting for the *Meyerkord* to pull in from deployment. I was walking down the sidewalk on base, and I saw someone in khakis coming from the other direction. As he got closer, I was ready to salute him because I thought he was an officer, but when I got closer, my jaw dropped. It was Chief Surdez! Or should I say, "Master 'Chief' Surdez?"

He looked at me with a big grin and said, "Well, I'll be dipped in shit! If it isn't Boot Camp! What the fuck are you doing here?"

I told him I was in the transient barracks, waiting on my ship.

"So, what the fuck do they have you doing?" he asked.

"Well, mostly cleaning the barracks," I told him.

"That's bullshit!" he said. "Come with me."

We walked to his office at the fleet headquarters. He got on the phone to the transient barracks, talked a little bit, hung up, and said, "You work for me now."

The rest of my time in transit was awesome. At first, I'd go to his office in the morning, do some filing, but mostly just shoot the shit with him.

About lunchtime, he'd tell me, "I don't have anything else for you to do. Why don't you just go on liberty?"

It was great! After about a week, I went into his office in the morning (no set time), and he asked me, "You wanna go to school, Boot Camp?"

"What school?" I asked.

"Well, there's a five-inch gun maintenance course over on mainside. I can get you in if you want. It's a two-week course and will probably help you when you get to your ship."

"Sure!" I said.

So, the next thing I knew, I was in the five-inch maintenance course. Master chiefs have a lot of clout. I would have given anything in the world if Master Chief Surdez could have been at my chief's initiation. I lost touch with him after running into him in San Diego and have tried repeatedly to locate him, but never have been able to. He was like a dad to me and the greatest role model a young man could have.

## Fair Winds and Following Seas

My last duty station was at Fleet Training Group, Pearl Harbor, Hawaii. It was good duty, plus I got to stay in Hawaii. I became the instructor for the Pacific Fleet Magazine Sprinkler Inspector Course, but also, I was assigned to be an inspector/instructor to go aboard ships for "refresher training."

Periodically, all navy and coast guard ships have to go through "refresher training." It lasts about three weeks and is pretty intensive. When a ship enters REFTRA, the command of the ship is turned over to the commodore of the fleet training group. At the beginning, inspectors (all either petty officers first class, chief petty officers, senior chief petty officers, and master chief petty officers) go aboard the ship and do an inspection. The inspection includes going over all the ship's records and a physical inspection of the machinery and equipment.

Next, FTG conducts drills, general quarters, firefighting, security, navigation, engineering, and gunnery, just to name a few. The inspectors observe all the drills and the proficiency of the crew. Then the observers brief the captain and department heads on what they observe and offer recommendations for improvement. After all the training is finished, the ship is put through one final battle problem, which consists of a simulated battle scenario, where the ship takes "hits" from enemy gunfire, torpedoes, aircraft, or missiles.

Everything is observed and graded, from the weapons' responses to fire team proficiency. It usually lasts most of the day, and at the end, a final grade is established and the captain and department heads are briefed. Most ships improved during the course of REFTRA, but some didn't. I've seen a few fail. If that happens, the ship has to go through it all over again.

Whenever we reported aboard a ship, we were always treated with respect. Generally, the food we were served was excellent, because the cooks would put their best foot forward in order to make a good impression. Coast guard ships were the best at this. We'd wake up in the morning to coffee and donuts, then a big breakfast. Then throughout the day, if we went to the chiefs' mess, we'd find snacks laid out for us, even smoked salmon. I loved riding the coastie ships. Also, they were pretty well trained and took a lot of pride in their jobs.

The only exception I ever saw to this was a small oceangoing tug I was assigned to. The day I walked aboard to start my inspection; I was *not* impressed. The ship was equipped with a single, manually operated, slow-fire three-inch gun mount and a couple of .50-caliber machine guns. I started my inspection on the three-inch gun, and what I found just about made my hair curl. Just about every movable part of the gun was seized up from rust and lack of lubrication. I couldn't even get the breech open. Then I checked the .50 caliber machine guns. They were in about the same condition. Rust everywhere, and the headspace and timing were way off. I tried to unscrew the barrel to set the headspace, but it wouldn't budge. I questioned the gunner's mate first class, and the response I got was that the gunner's mates just didn't have enough time to do all the maintenance.

When I briefed the captain on my findings, he was shocked and assured me that he was going to get to the bottom of it. This was on a Friday. We were supposed to get underway on Monday for exercises. Monday morning, I reported back aboard. The first thing I did was to reinspect the gun mount. I guess a miracle happened over the weekend. The gun was clean; everything was freed up; and the breech wasn't rusty, had plenty of grease, and operated smoothly. Then I checked the .50 calibers. They were clean, rust-free, and I was able to unscrew the barrels. I'm thinking that "somehow" the gunner's mates found time over the weekend to do the job they should have been doing all along.

I was told later by one of the chiefs that the captain and the gunner's mate first class had a long heart-to-heart conversation on Friday. I don't think the gunner's mates saw very much of Honolulu that weekend. Also, I don't think they liked me very much; they didn't have much to say to me while I was on board. That was okay though. I'd rather they'd be safe than popular. Even the smallest, slowest gun mount can kill you if you don't nurture it properly.

As an observer/inspector, I would be assigned to a ship for the duration they were in REFTRA. Whenever the ship got underway, I'd go with it to do training for the gunnery division. It was sometimes pretty grueling with some pretty long days. We would mess with the ship's chiefs, and if space permitted, we'd berth in the chief's quarters; if not, we'd berth with the crew. I had the opportunity to ride a lot of ships, both navy and coast guard, and train a lot of sailors. When a ship's in REFTRA, it's probably underway about 90 percent of the time, so even though I was stationed ashore, I was still going to sea a lot. Whenever I wasn't assigned to a ship, I taught regular classroom courses at our headquarters on Ford Island in Pearl Harbor. I had to ride a small boat back and forth to work every day, which wasn't bad. I didn't have to deal with traffic, and it was actually pretty relaxing.

While I was attached to FTG, the command didn't have any gunner's mates that were qualified on the "then new" Mark 75, 76 mm Otto-Melara gun mount. I ended up being chosen to go to the school at the Naval Ordnance Station, in Louisville,

Kentucky. The school was a month long, and they had an actual gun mount there.

It was a pretty good course. I learned everything about the gun system, but in my opinion, as a gunner's mate, it was a piece of crap. Apparently, it was originally designed in Italy and bought by the United States, then it was modified to meet our safety standards. Even with the modifications we did, it was still a "man-eater."

There were so many different things that were dangerous about it. With stored energy in the loader arms, if you were doing maintenance and weren't careful, the arms could cycle and take your arm off or worse. The firing cutouts were screwy, and there was the possibility of firing into the ship's superstructure. It was a fast gun, I'll admit, but a dangerous one. I completed the course, got the enlisted classification for it, and returned to Pearl Harbor. After that, any ships that went through REFTRA that had a 76 mm gun mount were assigned to me.

The Naval Ordnance Station in Louisville was pretty impressive. They took my class on a tour of it, and I got to see how they made sixteen-inch gun barrels, the barrels for the guns on battleships. The biggest lathes I've ever seen. Louisville itself was interesting. I went to the Jim Beam distillery, the Kentucky Fried Chicken Museum, and Fort Knox with the Patton Museum.

An interesting thing happened to me as I was flying back to Hawaii from Kentucky. I was traveling in my uniform, in my dress khakis, and after the plane landed in Honolulu, everyone was getting out of their seats and getting their carry-on bags. I grabbed my briefcase and stepped out into the aisle, and a couple rows forward, I let an airline pilot, who was traveling as a passenger, step out in front of me; it was the polite thing to do.

He looked at me and said, "You should be ashamed of yourself!"

"Why?" I asked, totally bewildered.

He gestured to the ribbons on my chest and said, "You need to take those off. You were never in Vietnam. You weren't old enough. You're too young to have been there."

He was referring to my Vietnam Campaign and Vietnam Service ribbons.

I looked him in the eye and said, "I was there in 1972 when I was seventeen years old. Go fuck yourself!"

He didn't say another word. I guess he missed my Good Conduct ribbon with three stars. I would never wear an award I didn't earn. Some guys do, and I think it's disgusting. When I was an instructor at gunnery school, there was a fellow instructor who had a chest full of ribbons, including a Seal eagle and trident. He probably had six or seven rows. He was full of war stories and claimed he had been a Seal. The students loved him because he'd tell stories during class time instead of teaching.

We also had another instructor, a very professional petty officer first class and an excellent instructor. He got suspicious about the validity of the other instructor's stories and went to our chief, who went to the personnel office and pulled his service record. The next day this guy got called into the director's office. When he came out, all his ribbons and insignia were gone. The next morning, he showed up with two ribbons, a Good Conduct and a National Defense. He was pretty much ostracized after that. Nobody wanted to have anything to do with him, including the students. In my book, stolen valor is a pretty serious offense, especially to people who actually earned it.

My naval career was to come to an end while I was at the fleet training group. Unfortunately, I developed some medical problems that made me unfit for duty. The Medical Review Board declined my request to remain on active duty, and thus, I was discharged. I had served seventeen and a half years, almost to retirement, but fell short. After the board made their decision, I was discharged within three days. Going out into the civilian world was scary for me. I had ridden destroyers my entire adult life and faced a lot of dangers and hardships, but being a civilian was the scariest thing I ever did.

# Glossary

All branches of the military have their own unique language. None more so than the navy. Naval language and terms come from centuries of seafarers. It can be very difficult for a landlubber (someone who's never been to sea) to understand what a sailor is talking about, so I'm providing a glossary to translate.

**abeam**—off to the left or right; 90 degrees or 270 degrees from the ship's course.

**aft**—behind.

**bearing**—a point on the compass, also a point relative to the ships course; 0° at the bow, then clockwise for 360° back to the bow.

**below**—inside the ship from the main deck down.

**berth**—a bed; can also mean where a ship is docked.

**bit**—a round, mushroom-shaped fixture that is attached to the deck, to which mooring lines are attached.

**bow**—the front, or pointy end, of a ship.

**bridge**—the command center of a ship; where the ship is steered from.

**broom**—a broom.

**brow**—the gangway used to board a ship; always gives on to the quarterdeck.

**bulkhead**—a wall on a ship.

**chock**—an oval hole attached to the main deck that mooring lines are threaded through.

**CIC (Combat Information Center)**—a room attached to the bridge of a ship where all tactical data is available for the mission of the ship. All radar, sonar, target, and course information are plotted here.

**cover**—your hat.

**deck**—the floor.

**foc'sle**—see *forecastle*.

**forecastle**—also called a foc'sle; the weather deck at the pointy end of a ship.

**fantail**—the rear main weather deck of a ship.

**galley**—a ship's kitchen.

**geedunk**—any kind of snack or candy; can also mean where such things are sold, such as a snack bar.

**goat locker**—where the chiefs live.

**hatch**—a door.

**head**—a bathroom.

**horse cock**—bologna

**Irish pennant**—a loose thread on your uniform.

**liberty**—when a sailor is allowed to go ashore for time off.

**light locker**—a vestibule given to the outside of a ship, equipped with black canvas screens to prevent white light from escaping at night.

**line**—a rope.

**magazine**—where a ship's ammunition is stored. Also, a rectangular holder for bullets, which is inserted into a rifle or pistol.

**mess**—a place to eat.

**midrats**—small meals served at midnight for the offgoing and oncoming watch.

**muster**—roll call.

**officers' country**—where the officers' staterooms are located (stay out of there).

**overhead**—the ceiling.

**passageway**—a hallway on a ship.

**pilot house**—the bridge.

**plan of the day**—a schedule of a ship's tentative evolutions for the day; published every evening and distributed throughout the ship and read to the entire crew at morning quarters.

**pollywog**—a crew member who's never been across the equator.

**quarterdeck**—the place where you board a ship; where the brow is; a sacred place, manned by an officer of the deck, a petty officer of the watch, and a messenger of the watch (watches rotate every four hours).

**quarters**—morning formation for muster, instruction, and inspection; also the compartment in which you live.

**rack**—a bed.

**rain locker**—a shower.

**rat guard**—a conical guard placed on mooring lines to keep rats from boarding a ship.

**running lights**—ships at sea are required to show lights at night so other ships can determine the course and speed of each other to prevent collisions: a white masthead light visible all the way around, a white stern light (visible only from the stern), a red port light (visible only from the front of the ship to the port beam), and a green light on the starboard side (visible only from the front of the ship to the starboard beam).

**salt**—an experienced sailor.

**scullery**—where they wash dishes.

**scuttle**—a small, round hatch; can also mean to intentionally sink one's own ship.

**shellback**—a crew member who's been across the equator before.

**sliders**—hamburgers.

**small stuff**—rope that is quarter inch in circumference or smaller.

**snot locker**—your nose.

**stern**—the back end of a ship.

**surf and turf**—steak and lobster (occasionally).

**swab**—a mop.

**topside**—anywhere outdoors from the main deck up.

**tube steaks**—hot dogs.

**vestibule**—a small room approximately four feet by four feet; all hatches that give to the outside of a ship have vestibules. There is an inner door and an outer hatch—this is to keep white light from showing when you access the weather decks at night.

**wardroom**—where the officers eat.

**water line**—a line on a ship's hull where the water starts. All of the ship's hull below the water line is the ship's "draft."

www.ingramcontent.com/pod-product-compliance
Lightning Source LLC
Chambersburg PA
CBHW061519050726
47593CB00002B/645